AF530469

Writing Nation's History

Writing Nation's History

A Study of Three Postcolonial Texts

Amar Mishra

RAWAT PUBLICATIONS
Jaipur • New Delhi • Bangalore • Hyderabad • Guwahati • Kolkata

ISBN 978-81-316-0663-6

© Author, 2014

No part of this book may be reproduced or transmitted in any form or by any means, electronic or mechanical, including photocopying, recording or by any information storage and retrieval system, without permission in writing from the publishers.

Published by
Prem Rawat for **Rawat Publications**
Satyam Apts, Sector 3, Jawahar Nagar, Jaipur 302 004 (India)
Phone: 0141 265 1748 / 7006 Fax: 0141 265 1748
E-mail: info@rawatbooks.com
Website: www.rawatbooks.com

New Delhi Office
4858/24, Ansari Road, Daryaganj, New Delhi 110 002
Phone: 011 2326 3290

Also at *Bangalore, Hyderabad, Guwahati* and *Kolkata*

Typeset by Rawat Computers, Jaipur

Printed at Chaman Enterprises, New Delhi

Dedicated to
Goddess Samaleswari and my Parents

Contents

Acknowledgement

I thank Professor Jasbir Jain to have written a very insightful Foreword for the book. I thank Dr P.N. Mishra, Professor Sumanyu Satpathy and Professor Moonmoon Mazumdar for their timely advice and guidance in completing this book. Finally I thank all my family members for their support all through this project.

Foreword

The work in my hand by Dr Amar Mishra captures my response through its plural thrust. The novels selected represent a chronological shift as well as one in location. Rushdie looks back in a post-view of history and brings it to the present, engaging with both political and social history. *Midnight's Children* opens a new discourse on the subcontinent.

Moving on to *A Suitable Boy*, the approach has to open out into more realistic concerns of class, relationships and economy. Seth has been periodically an at-home writer, before making up his mind in favour of the west. His vision does not hold the nostalgia that Rushdie disguises as magic realism in his work; instead Seth places his approach in irony, thus distancing himself from his subject to obtain a long distance perspective.

The third text by Roy shifts further South and is concerned with caste, religion and gender; it seeks to adopt a stylistic method of distancing, through a web of language and memory. The playfulness of the beginning continues to deepen itself gradually to culminate in tragedy as religion and the inhumanity of man are contrasted, as they dwell together in the human mind and heart. All three writers take off into different trajectories in concern, style, narration and location. Spread over a period of twenty years, between them they cover more than a span of fifty years through memory, nostalgia, biographical pasts and the interplay of events. In how many ways is the nation constructed? How do politics and economy interweave? What finally is the relation between the shifting locales, the issues of policy and the individual and tradition and modernity?

All of the above compel us to explore the unexplored dimensions of both history and postcoloniality. Does the postcolonial extend or go beyond its initial concept? Does it move into post colony and shake itself free finally of the 'post', or are we to content ourselves with Bhabha's concept of cultural hybridity? One begins to realise that sooner than later, the creative writer begins to leave both the critic and the theorist behind – it is not theory which generates creativity but creativity which challenges it. The nation in India is a plural construct, and it is this plurality which is reflected here. The measure of a work is reflected in its ability to interrogate and then provoke the reader to interrogate further. Having been extended the courtesy of being invited to write the Foreword, I happen to be the first interrogator and hope there are many more.

Jasbir Jain

1 Defining Colonialism/Postcolonialism as a Literary Theory and its Applications

Critical Survey of India as a Material for Fiction Writing

The Oxford English Dictionary defines the word 'colonialism' as something coming from the Roman word 'colonia', which means 'farm or settlements especially of the Romans outside their own country, but still retaining their citizenship'. It can be called as a settlement in a country forming a community subject to or still connected to their parent state.

The above definition refers to the colonizers only and it does not refer to the people who might be living there while the colony was being established. Hence, there is no virtual conflict between the colonizers and the original inhabitants. It is often seen that the process of colonizing or forming a community for that matter in any new land involves recognising the communities that already existed there. It also involved practices like trade, plunder, negotiations, warfare, genocide, enslavement and rebellion. Therefore, colonialism can be defined as the forceful domination of other people's land and economy. This is something which has surfaced in different forms in different ages. It was not merely the expansion of European powers into Asia, Africa or for that matter any other country, but it has been a recurring theme ever since the beginning of human history. It was found in the second century AD that the Roman Empire stretched from Armenia to the Atlantic. Similarly, many other empires under many rulers had occupied lands far away from their own. this phenomenon was applicable to various kingdoms within India too, especially in South India we find it was under the Vijayanagara Empire. Also the Ottoman Empire, which was quite insignificant in the beginning, was able to extend over most of Asia up to the Balkans.

The establishment of colonies by different powers has not left any part of the globe untouched. It is often considered that the Mughals were the fuel for the Europeans' journey to different parts of the world. In order to understand the success of the European powers in establishing colonies, we need to clarify a few important questions. The most important is, whether they were a superior race? These Europeans who came to establish colonies in Africa, Australia or even in India always looked down upon the original inhabitants as 'others' and referred to themselves as 'us'. These two words 'other' and 'us' ushered in a large gap between the colonizers and the colonized. The colonizers always took care to see that there was a complex relationship between the colonized and themselves so that there was a constant flow of humans and natural resources between the colonized and colonial countries.

There was a situation created in such a manner that the colonized always remained subdued and trampled. The European colonizers employed many ways of domination, whereby they penetrated deep into some of the societies, having a superficial contact with others. Thus, it can be said that colonialism helped in the growth of European capitalism. In other words, we can say that colonialism helped in the formation of a capitalist Europe. Colonialism is also referred to as imperialism, where, according to the OED, imperial means simply 'pertaining to empire' and imperialism means 'rule of the Emperor'.

Colonialism helped in the growth of European industry, hence capital was arranged or achieved through colonial domination, and imperialism is the highest form of colonialism. A distinction in the modern sense may be drawn between colonialism as the takeover of territory, appropriation of natural resources, exploitation of labour and interference with political and cultural structures of another nation and imperialism as a global system (Loomba, 1998: 6). The imperial system is just defined as a political system of governance and the imperial centre governs countries. But the postcolonial situation signals the end of the imperial system of governance, or the collapse of imperialism after a country is declared independent. If imperialism is taken to be an economic system of penetrating the market, then the political changes do not affect it in any manner. It may also be redefined as in case of the American imperialism which has abundant resources, money and military power across the globe without direct political control. It can also be perceived that although there is some kind of link between imperialism and colonialism, there are also differences which can be defined separately, depending upon their historical mutations. But in any case, both imperialism and colonialism are a process that leads to domination and control over other people's land and economy. Therefore, what happened in colonies as a result of imperial domination is colonialism. Power flows out of the imperial centre, but 'imperialism' can function without formal colonies, whereas colonialism cannot (ibid., 1998: 7). The Europeans, by journeying to different parts of the globe, were able to create a class of people, especially in the East (India), whom they called the Orientals and ruled for more than two centuries. They called themselves Occidentals and also justified their forceful domination. They claimed that the Orientals were feminine, weak, emotional, sentimental and superstitious, whereas the Occidentals on the other hand were much superior class of people. They considered themselves as masculine, rational and disciplined (Said, 2001). Further, Edward Said also writes that 'The Orientals were linked to elements in Western society (delinquents, the insane, woman, the poor) having in common an identity best described as lamentably alien. Orientals were rarely seen or looked at: they were seen through, analysed not as citizens, or even people, but as problems to be solved or confined or – as the colonial powers openly coveted their territory – taken over' (ibid., p. 207).

In colonialism, another important feature is the racial difference of colour. Colour plays an important role, because in most of the colonies established, whiteness and wealth dovetailed. It clearly did not do so within European countries, where working class were free to display any amount of racism as their masters. According to the Prime Minister of Cape Colony (1908), white workers were delighted on arrival to find themselves in a position of an aristocracy of colour (mark of superiority). Many writers have expressed colonialism in different forms. Frantz Fanon writes in his book *Black Skin, White Masks*, that the colonized people are not simply those whose labour has been appropriated, but those in whose soul an 'inferiority complex has been created by the death and burial of its local cultural originality' (1967: 81). Similarly, Italian communist Antonio Gramsci opines that colonialism is 'the preliterate or the oppressed class or subject possessing a dual consciousness, that which is beholden to a resistance'. The process of colonialism leads to another feature called 'hegemony', which means forceful domination by some external force. This domination may be upon, anything be it land, economy, literature, or culture of social standing. According to Antonio Gramsci, 'hegemony', is power achieved through the combination of coercion and consent. He also states that the ruling class achieved domination not by force or by coercion but by creating subjects who 'willingly', submitted to being ruled. Hence, we can say that the role of ideology is very important, because it helps in creating consent among the people. It also acts as a medium through which certain ideas are transmitted, held to be true. It is often seen that commonsense of the people also has a great deal to contribute towards the growth of hegemony, because hegemony is achieved by plying with the commonsense of the people. Italian philosopher Antonio Gramsci has come out with a view that racism is not just an effect of capitalism, but is more complexly intertwined with it. He has further influenced researchers worldwide with his work that postcolonial domination involved much repression, and this is sometimes analysed as a system that perhaps did not involve any kind of consent of the colonized.

II

Unlike the word 'colonialism', the word 'postcolonialism' is a bit complicated in the sense of the term 'post'. In ancient times, things were not well organised and the descendents of the coloured people lived everywhere. In this sense, the whole world is postcolonial (Loomba, 1998: 7). According to Ania Loomba, the prefix 'post' complicates because it implies to all those countries which were once colonized or to the people who have been out of the clutches of colonialism and imperialism. Both the terms are often interchangeably used, and in this sense it makes the whole world colonial. Since it is found that the whole world is colonial in its attitude and style of functioning, the other aspects of the word 'post' and 'colonial' are viewed separately. However, there is no problem with the word 'post' but the word 'colonial', which reveals that after colonialism the postcolonial societies were habituated with living in a colonial world. In this context, 'colonial discourse' assumes a great deal of significance. Edward Said, the author of the famous book *Orientalism*, points out that the extent to which 'knowledge' about the 'orient' was produced and circulated in Europe was an ideological accompaniment of colonial power. This book is not about the non-western cultures, particularly in the scholarly discipline called 'Orientalism'. Said shows how the discipline of Orientalism was created alongside the European penetration of the Near-East, and how it was nurtured and supported by various other disciplines, such as philology, history, anthropology, philosophy, archaeology and literature.

According to Valerie Kennedy, defining Orientalism seems to be a complex and contradictory business. Edward Said's definition of the Orient and Orientalism is that Orientalism is a discourse in Michel Foucault's meaning of the term. Edward Said views the basics of Orientalism in three aspects. Firstly, it is an academic tradition of study, teaching and writing about the Orient. Second, it is a style of thought based on the ontological and epistemological distinction made between the 'Orient' and the 'Occident'. Third, it is the corporate institution for dealing with the 'Orient', or a

Western style for dominating, restructuring and having authority over the 'Orient' (2001: 21). According to Edward Said, Orientalism is said to inaugurate a new kind of study of colonialism. Said argues that representation of the 'Orient' in European literary texts, travelogues and other writings contributed to the creation of a dichotomy that was central to the creation of European culture as well as to the maintenance and extension of European hegemony over other lands. Said also shows how knowledge about non-Europeans was part of the process of maintaining power over them. Then the status of knowledge is demystified and the lines between the knowledge about the East could never be objective, because it was produced by human beings, who were necessarily embedded in colonial history and relationship. But it was Frantz Fanon who much before Edward Said had opined that it was Europe that was responsible for the creation of the 'Third World'. They got materials, wealth and labour from the colonies, leading to such human sufferings as the sweat and dead bodies of Negroes, Arabs, Indians and the yellow race.

Edward Said's basic thesis is that Orientalism or the study of the Orient was ultimately a political vision of reality whose structure promoted a binary opposition between the familiar Europe; the West and us, and the stranger; the Orient (East and them). Said also writes that the opposition to the Europeans was always crucial, if colonised people are irrational, the Europeans are rational; if the former are barbaric, sensual and lazy, then Europe stands for civilization itself. If the Orient is static, Europe can be seen marching ahead and developing. The Orient is viewed as feminine but Europe is associated with masculinity.

'Orientalism' refers to ways how the Orient was constructed by the Western literature, travel writings and system of studying the East, and not with how a construction was received or dismantled by the colonial subjects. 'Colonial discourse' is not just a fancy new term for colonialism. It indicates a new way of thinking in which cultural, intellectual, economic or political processes are seen to work together in the formation, perpetuation and dismantling of colonialism.

According to scholars, objectivity alone does not account for claiming ideological and political innocence. Humanist literary studies have resisted the idea that literature has anything to do with politics on the grounds that the former is too subjective, individual or personal. The relationship between literature and colonialism was not taken seriously by literary criticism. But in recent times, the role of this relationship has been considered with a great deal of importance. Literature circulates in society and it does a great job for the colonizers. It creates a cultural authority both in the metros and in the colonies. Literature acts as the contact zone, where transfer of culture takes place in all its complexities. Finally, it can be said that literature is quite important with regard to the means of appropriating, inventing or challenging dominant means of representation and colonial ideology. Hence, there is a kind of interaction between literature and colonialism. During the European Renaissance, there were numerous tales of travellers which were an amalgamation of fiction, attitudes received from earlier times, and new observations. But there was no fixed interpretation of what they saw and encountered. Hence, the Black Africans were termed bestial, both in terms of their colour and also because of the association of blackness with dirt and filth. Thus, they gave ample reason for the colonials to colonise and enslave them.

The nationalism practised in England basically relied on the cultural distinctions that demarcated Europeans from the Blacks. There was a strong line of distinction drawn between the coloured classes of people. This demarcation justified an aggressive nationalism which triggered England's overseas expansion. Therefore, it is very often seen that language and literature played a very important role in the creation of the European 'self', and the non-European 'other'. Edward Said suggested that this is a part of the creation of the colonial authority (Loomba, 1998: 73). There was another aspect of the role of language and literature during the colonial period. Peter Hulme, in his work on the formation of colonial discourse in the sixteenth century, highlights the fact that just to strengthen an ideological discourse, two words 'cannibal' and 'hurricane' were lifted from the Native American language and adopted as new words by all major European languages (ibid.). These two words highlighted by Hulme not only suggest two new meanings, but they demarcate the boundary between Europe and America, between civility and wilderness. The word 'cannibal' indicates the 'threat' that the savages could turn against and eat the Europeans.

III

These words highlighted by Hulme indicated all that happened in Europe. The word 'cannibal' has a deeper meaning. It is linked to highlight the pseudo-nature or the semi-dark character of the non-Europeans. Do writings which highlight the dark side of the non-Europeans depict only the dark side of the non-Europeans or they also depict the dehumanisation of colonial rule? Texts like *The Tempest* and *Othello* written by William Shakespeare have been read differently by different people. *The Tempest* was accepted as a romantic piece of writing and it had nothing to do with colonialism. But recently it has been taken by many critics as an anti-colonial text, as it deals with the struggles of the enslaved Caliban. European writings had a great impact on the East, the people and their cultures, including that of the colonized. But the non-Western writing, that of the East, was not developed in isolation but was shaped by the foreign, including colonial encounters (ibid., p. 75). There are many books written based on the facts that they shall be an eye-opener for the West regarding the East.

O. Chandu Menon's *Indulekha* was written after the author's wife expressed her desire to read a novel written on the English fashion, and to see whether the Indian native writer could create that kind of writing among the native population, not conversant with English. George Lemming's essay published in 1960 clearly indicates that literature plays an important role both in developing and controlling colonial subjects and in countering the colonial forces, or in challenging colonialism. Similarly, there are many more books written both by foreign writers and Indian natives like Salman Rushdie, Vikram Seth, Raja Rao and Arundhati Roy whose texts maybe studied critically from the point of view of 'postcolonialism' as a literary theory. Among the foreign authors, we have Frantz Fanon, Chinua Achebe, and Joseph Conrad, whose books have generated a lot of critical response for 'postcolonial' study.

Frantz Fanon, who is a major contributor to colonial/postcolonial studies, has written an important book *Black Skin, White Masks* (1952), that this is partly a manifesto, partly an analysis. The book represents Fanon's personal experience as a black intellectual in a white world and elaborates the ways in which the colonized-colonizer relationship is normalised as psychology. Fanon also writes that racism generates harmful psychological constructs that both blind the black man to his subjection to a universalized white norm and alienates his consciousness. According to Fanon, blackness is associated with evil, hence the black man dons a white mask or thinks a universal subject equally participating in the activities of the society. Similarly, Joseph Conrad writes in his book *Heart of Darkness* (1902) on matters other than sea fearing, river boating and exploration. He also writes about imperialism and colonialism, race relations and also about the mysteries of the subconscious mind.

The book written by Chinua Achebe titled *Things Fall Apart* is central not only in African literature, but also in postcolonial literary and cultural discourse. He inaugurated a long and continuing tradition of inquiry into the problematic relations between the West and the nations of the Third World.

There is always an interrelatedness of the literary with the non-literary texts. The relation of both to colonial discourse can be unravelled. There are many representations where we find the Occidentals calling themselves masters and the Orientals, being projected in a feminine form. Here Said observes that the Occidentals thought themselves to be more superior to the Orientals. Dark skin represents colonized, but white skin colonizers, and they also represent Europe. But in the book *The Tempest* written by William Shakespeare, there is a complete reversal of the general order. Here, a white skinned woman, an

Occidental, is threatened of rape by a black skinned Oriental. This reverses the allegation of colonialism as rape to some extent. Thus, this is one of the reasons for the deflection of violence of the colonial encounter from the colonizers to the colonized.

A representation of the dark skinned people as rapists in all forms of literary writings was a commonplace thinking of the Europeans. It was a false pretext to camouflage their own sense of guilt. Literature and history combined produced a stereotype of the exiting colonial elements. This was a kind of creation from within, and especially after the uprising of 1857, which led to the transformation of the mild Hindu to someone else, as someone who projects himself as the rapist of all white women. There were no such reports before the mutiny of 1857, but all the stories surfaced only after the revolt against the colonial power. It was all because this uprising was able to shake the British Empire from within. Though the British Empire was shaken, there is no written document of any systematic violence after the uprising. But the provoking stories made things real and helped in giving a particular shape. Hence the idea of truth-effects, where discourse can produce the same effects as actual events is Foucaultian in origin and it is useful in expressing the material effects of ideology without conflicting the two (Loomba, 1998: 80). Loomba also suggests that there are a range of novels about India which play with the history of the country. For example, E.M. Forster's *A Passage to India* also plays with history and exemplifies the general order of the European superiority over the Orientals. But, the novel accuses an Indian man of raping a British woman, even though the novel was written much later in the year 1920 after the massacre of Jallianwala Bagh where hundreds of Indians were ruthlessly butchered by the British forces under the command of Brigadier General Dyer. This event had openly challenged the colonial regime in India. Paul Scott, another very famous author of the book *The Jewel in the Crown,* also highlights the colonial element being raped by an Indian man. The book highlights rape as a metaphor of imperialism.

All the chronologies put together form a kind of misunderstanding that literary and cultural theory has widened the scope of studies on colonialism. It has also created a problem for a historically specific materialist critical practice. Ania Loomba exhaustively writes that both Homi Bhabha and Gayatri C. Spivak have been accused of an exorbitation of discourse, of neglecting material conditions of colonial rule by concentrating on colonial representation. She also suggests that this tendency has to do with the fact that what is circulated as 'postcolonial' theory has largely emerged from within English literary studies.

The postcolonial theory deals with the reading and writing of literature that was written previously or currently by countries which deal with colonialism or the colonized people. It mainly focuses on the way in which literature by a colonising culture distorts the experience and realities and inscribes the inferiority of the colonized people. It was also found that literature by the colonized people, attempts to articulate their identity and reclaim their past in the face of the past's inevitable 'otherness'. This 'otherness' can also deal with the way in which literature in the colonizing countries appropriates the language, images and scenes, the traditions and so forth of those colonized countries. Furthermore, the postcolonial theory is built in large part around the concept of 'otherness', but at the same time it was also seen that this otherness had a great impact on the lives of the colonized people.

The colonial forces moved into new landscapes, established new founding national myths, and struggled to define their own national literature against the very force and tradition of the British. They themselves were of British or European heritage, but ultimately encountered the originating traditions as 'other', a tradition and a writing to define one's self against (or which amounts to the same thing). Every colony had an emerging literature which was an imitation of, but different from the central British tradition, which also articulated in local terms the myths and experiences of a new culture. It was also something which expressed that new culture as divergent from and even opposed to the culture of the home or the colonizing nations.

It was also found that the colonizers largely inhabited the countries which absorbed the peoples of a number of other heritages and cultures, through immigration, migration or the forced mingling of different local cultures. In doing so, they adapted the use of myth, symbols and definitions of various traditions. In this way, the literature of the hitherto colonizers became postcolonial.

Although the postcolonial literature is that colonialist literature being an attempt to replicate, continue, equal the original tradition to write in accordance with the literature of otherness and resistance, it is written completely out of specific local experience (Lye, 1997).

IV

The transfer of power from a colonial to postcolonial situation was not a smooth one-instead, it was accompanied by pain, violence and suffering. It gave rise to new configurations and new histories. Out of it surfaced suppressed memories and fanned hatred and hostilities as millions of people were displaced. The independence of India also changed the relationship of the intellectuals to the establishment. All the major writers of the period were involved in the struggle for freedom. According to Dharmavir Bharati, this period was one of uprooting and unsettlement. Before the partition, the leaders were united by a common bond despite all political differences but these things were fast becoming things of the past.

Dislocation of people is a global phenomenon, especially as huge populations are dislocated due to war, or be it the Nazi preoccupation, the Nagasaki-Hiroshima blasts and the liquidation of the imperial powers. The partition of the country was also a period which brought about traditional loyalties, territorial claims and religious afflictions into conflict. No colonization is ever terminated by a stroke of a pen. There is no finality in its termination, primarily because it has infiltrated the lives and minds of people in multiple ways. The past with its history and experience persists and continues to be a constant reminder, keeping in view all things related. This phase can be labelled as a postcolonial one.

It has become quite a convenient term for clubbing together the literature of the Third World and the erstwhile colonizers and more recently, also the works of the Black writers and immigrant population. This literature has been defined in many ways as resistance literature, as literature dating back after the encounter with an alien power, as literature requiring a different set of principles, or as one which gives voice to the marginalised. To name a few from the long list of writers who have contributed in the field of colonial and postcolonial literature are Frantz Fanon, Edward Said, Gayatri C. Spivak and Homi Bhabha. There are critics like Bill Ashcroft, Gareth Griffith, Helen Tiffin and many more. The list is quite exhaustive and this gives an evidence of the fact that there is a continued interest in the term despite its colossal structure. Moreover, there is also an Indian connection to it.

The literature that was formed after the colonial period marked some radical changes. It was seen that very often the relationship between the two classes developed during the colonial period, the 'self' and 'other'. They were in constant conflict, distrust, hostilities and suspension. Colonialism employs a strategy of subordination and appropriation and it uses linguistic imposition and religious conversion as a means of controlling the native identity. But postcolonialism works through a search of alternatives such as alternative history, alternative education and alternative modernity. Colonialism is said to have changed the entire ethos of the colonizers and the colonized.

Postcolonialism or postcolonial literature is a direct contrast to colonialism's policy of subordination and ensures looking for equality and an articulation of differences. The relationship of the colonizers and the colonized is something which is characterised by power and the production of knowledge. Great philosophers and thinkers like Marx and Mill were also committed to equality of all races, but they also justified the White rule over the 'barbaric', coloured world. Postcolonial strategies sought to resurrect the past, to anchor the 'self' in tradition.

According to some intellectuals, the history of postcolonialism began in India in the year 1857, with the First War of

Independence. The impact of colonialism was directed at rendering the native culture recessive and imposing the normative patterns of the western world, but, postcolonialism had to work in the opposite direction to assert all the cultural values, create a new 'self', and reform a divisive social system. History plays an important role in the postcolonial writings, especially in India, or when it comes to the Indian context. According to Bill Ashcroft, Gareth Griffiths and Helen Tiffin, the authors of *The Empire Writes Back,* history is a prominent feature of postcolonial writings (1989: 169–81). They also present an overall framework within which the question of history can be understood with regard to all postcolonial countries, including India.

Tiffin also stresses that history has a very important place and a specific role in the postcolonial writings, especially in India. She emphasises on the history-myth connection in very specific terms. In her view, the main thrust of postcolonial writings is to establish, or rehabilitate self against either European appropriation or rejection (Ashcroft, Griffiths and Tiffin, 1989: 172). Her main contention is that because the history of the erstwhile colonies was constructed, even fabricated by the colonizers mainly for justifying their presence, and repressive policies, the postcolonial writers challenge their 'master narratives' of history by fracturing them into two different ways, depending on the nature of the cultural system to which they belong.

These postcolonial writers used their indigenous resources in countries like Africa, Australia and India to challenge European perspectives. Inevitably, it is reflected in their conscious development of myth in all their writings (Dhar, 1996: 142). The best example that can be cited is Raja Rao's *Kanthapura*, where Rao tells a story of the incursion of western history into India from a perspective which constantly decentres the exploiters and foregrounds India and Indian systems (Tiffin, 1988: 175). Therefore, the postcolonial writers, who have cultural and metaphysical systems, fall back upon use of myth as a potent device for contesting the western ideology and the modes of representation. In the real sense, there is a constant struggle between colonial and postcolonial discourses, which is based on power and knowledge in the Foucaultian sense. Power is the conflicting factor, because it controls the production of knowledge and the knowledge so generated reinforces power.

The transfer of power from the colonial to postcolonial situation was not a simple one. There started a conflict between tradition and modernity, cohesiveness and plurality. There was also a continued displacement of people. The independence of India was not a mere transfer of the subjugated people to a free nation, but it was instrumental in breaking the cultural and traditional ethos of a nation which was split into two separate nations, with religion becoming a divisive factor. The position of India was a complete failure to safeguard the nation's will to stay united. The postcolonial period or the post-Independence period in India gave rise to different kinds of writings. We have literature related to Partition which projected problems on both sides of the border. They highlighted nation, space, community and administrative agencies. This literature was a projection of the pain, sufferings and the failure of human ideals and conversion of man to a bestial nature. The literature that came up during the postcolonial period worked in several different ways. But over and above, the novels that were written during the period, especially in India, explored history and interrogated the same for its hidden truths. The authors of these texts went back to the past to have a thorough scrutiny. There were also novels written which detailed the aftermath in terms of individual identities.

It is quite evident that the postcolonial period marked a drastic change in the writing of literature globally, very specifically in India. Both colonialism and postcolonialism are global phenomenon and shall not affect all countries alike. This global phenomenon affected all aspects of life, such as religion, which was considered to be an effective bond to keep things united. Language and attitude also mattered to a great extent. Ania Loomba writes that Amie Cesaire begins her book entitled *Discourse on Colonialism* thus: 'A civilization that proves incapable of solving her problems creates a decadent civilization. A civilization that chooses to close her eyes to the most crucial problems is a stricken civilization. A civilization that uses its principles for trickery and deceit is a dying civilization.' All the misdoings of the colonialists gave the colonized an upper hand, and also proves that the colonizers are weak.

The postcolonial period is a period of reckoning, because colonial subjects move from alienation to revolution, from recognition to injustice to resistance. From the historical point of view, anti-colonial resistance has taken many forms, and it must have been derived from many resources. The very process of colonialism has always reshaped, often violently, the physical territories, social terrains and human identities.

V

According to George Lamming, the effects of colonial experience can be well seen and felt especially in the Caribbean consciousness. The experience is something that concerns the psyche. Therefore, in order to challenge colonialism at all levels, a new kind of powerful identity is built up by the colonized people. It is an important thing to consider as to what extent the colonial powers succeeded in silencing the colonized. Because colonialism is always taken to be destructive in nature and the colonized are always the victims who are incapable of answering back. But, at the same time in the colonial period, the colonized wrote back (Ashcroft, Griffiths and Tiffin, 1989), and had the power to question the authority, in a way we are romanticising the very resistant subjects, underlying the colonial violence. The primary question is with regard to the language used by the Europeans. This is expressed by Gayatri Spivak: are the subaltern represented by the voice of the intellectual? But, in any case, these are not a part of the study of colonialism; still, it is quite crucial for any scholarship concerned with the recovery of past histories and perspectives of the marginalized people. These set of marginalized people may be women non-whites, non-Europeans, the lower classes and the oppressed castes or anyone who does not fall in the category of the Europeans. Hence, it must be ascertained as to what extent we are the products of dominant ideology, and how far we are such effective forces. These kinds of issues have been at the centrestage ever since Edward Said's *Orientalism* influenced the *postcolonial* studies. Of course, Edward Said's *Orientalism* has been a project which attempts to write histories from below or recovers the experiences of those who have been hidden from history, the so-called marginalized or the colonized people of the Third World. Before the coming of the British to India, it was under Muslim control. Unlike the British, these Muslims were not colonists, but they were simply termed immigrants from Central Asia. These Mughals who were ruling over most parts of India were foreigners. The whole of the Mughal rule rested upon a Hindu framework or mantle. In other words, the whole of the Mughal rule existed in terms of an undefined contract between the rulers and the ruled (Edwardes, 1967). It was observed that in some parts, Hindu rulers continued to administer their states as feudatories in exchange of circumscribed independence, supplying troops and also collecting revenue. Although many parts of India were under Muslim control, the South remained out of their clutches, but at the epicentre of Muslim power, there was widespread conversion. These conversions were for two reasons, one out of fear and second, to avoid being penalised by heavy taxes. All those who converted were from the unprivileged class of the society. But the extent of conversion in India is less when compared to other countries ruled by Muslims.

It is often observed that there is a wide gap between Islam and Hinduism. Rulers subsequently changed but the social conditions remained the same. The society was divided according to profession. The resultant factor was the loyalty of any class of people and it was towards their own group. The loyalty towards the state was subordinate and came only after own group. Even military service was the group concern of a professional caste; the people engaged in cultivation did not take part in wars. Although the Muslims were a class apart, they still had an exchange of ideas with Hindus. Urdu was an amalgam of the Hindus and the Muslims; it was an equivalent of Latin in Medieval Europe. In the latter part of the Mughal rule, the central administration began to crumble and the effects could be seen everywhere. It also affected the small

European trading settlements in India. These settlements were guaranteed protection by the Centre, but with the collapse of the Centre, the company officials wanted to arrange for their own defence. They began to fortify their settlements. Self-defence generated the necessity to occupy more territory than they had. This expansion of territory produced conflicts and participation in local politics. Further, with the collapse of the central administration, there was no organised system to take its place.

The British dominion spread slowly over India and all major areas were absorbed by 1856, although it met anarchy and chaos. In the whole process, force was the sole arbiter, and superior force backed by purpose which gained India for the British (British India, 1772–1947). Though the British took over most parts of India, in the South there was total chaos and anarchy. Bloodshed and murder was an everyday happening. There was a universal state of savage independence. There was all-round direct opposition to all regular governments. This again necessitated the annexation of a number of villages every year. The atmosphere in India was gradually becoming congenial for the British to take over, the grassroot settlement – the villages also fell to ruins and there was no cultivation. The only activity was that of tax collectors and robbers. There was an even situation everywhere in Punjab. It was seen that the system of governance set by Maharaja Ranjit Singh also dwindled, and it was also annexed by the British Empire in 1849. Before the imposition of British rule in India, and within the general chaos of life, there were certain continuities. The social order continued till the complete destruction of the village was over. Economic life, though disrupted, the production of goods continued at a level high enough to justify the interests of the European merchants. As observed by critics, the situation on the ground rather made it quite easy for the British takeover, even though the British did not feel secure or even were not convinced of the permanence of their dominion, even after fifty initial years in India. The British felt insecure but still did not allow their feelings to influence their action, so as to arouse any kind of opposition which they might fail to resist. The English men mostly enjoyed Indian luxuries. The initial relations with the Indians began to decline by the end of the century. It was because the British became conscious of the class superiority. This change in the social atmosphere began with the arrival of Lord Cornwallis in the year 1786. It was Cornwallis who had it in mind that each Indian is corrupt. Suddenly, it was found that the gap between the British and the Indians began to widen. When they started their expansion of the British society, the contribution to racial attitudes came from their society. Lord Cornwallis was succeeded by Lord Wellesley, who had nothing but contempt for the Indians. Another factor of rift between the British and the Indians was the English women. These women brought everything Christian. Thereby, the native mistresses were thrown aside by the British settlements. These native women were able to inject something of India into the world of the British. It was the influence of the Christian missionaries, although these missionaries mixed freely with the Indians. Still they called the Indians barbarous. They even convinced the British not to have a close relationship with the Indians. Gradually, it was found that the English society in all major towns and English settlements were able to supply all that was needed. The English began to create barriers that would ever further widen the gap. They began to fortify and construct fortresses into which they could retire after unwanted engagements with the native Indians. It was also found that by the year 1857, there developed a general idea among the British officials in India that the Indians are an evil lot and need to be ruled and civilized by Britain. The British had an imperial dream, because they had their eyes on the East. They believed that the East was a land of fables, a world of cinnamons, pearls, elephants and Nawabs.

Horace Walpole, the thinker and philosopher, had written that 'when we fall back in Europe, then we shall pack and move to India, and we shall rule again'. Walpole was a man of tremendous foresight and he could see things much before. In the same half century after the great battle of Waterloo, this was the measuring stick for the projector of Britain as highly defensive and separatist. It was where all her White colonies were concerned. This witnessed a burst of imperialism in the East. It brought the whole of India and South-East Asia into British control.

The British got ample scope to fulfil their ambition of establishing themselves on Indian soil, and this opportunity was created within India by India. It gave the British firm ground to justify their presence. It was also seen that the East, and especially India, was a ground for the British to blossom for the next three hundred years. It was after the break-up of the Mughal Empire that India was plunged into total chaos of warring states of brigandage, bloodshed and absolute corruption. The East India Company set up by the British as a trading base stood out like an oasis of order and comparative plenty.

Gradually, the old trend changed, the efficient system or organism swallowed the inefficient ones. The East India Company had even overrun some of the territory in the South, as they wanted to have one system throughout. But they had also left some of the land to be ruled by the native kings bound by a treaty. Although the Company spearheaded the process of occupation of place, the company cannot be called an aggressor. But gradually, the states were annexed to the British Empire; the process of annexation was quite well planned. The British as a whole community was baffled by the sudden uprising of the Bengal Army. They were of the impression that the slow reforms and progressive actions of the government had been able to arouse a sense of gratitude and affection among the Indians for the British. Suddenly, there was a turn of events and the gratitude was transformed to horror and all elements gave way to hatred and called for revenge. A sense of mistrust developed and though the British government was all for a policy of conciliation, many of the British were not. Though they realised that they were to be blamed for what had happened, the distrust never wholly disappeared. The British steadily increased their number, and they started leading a self-centred life with fewer contacts with the Indians. At times even if the situation warranted, the contact was purely official. They started to take less interest in the Indian culture and all things Indian. They almost became a separate caste, having several sub-castes, having strict control over their members. Gradually, it was found that the British came up with the railways which further widened the gap between the British and the Indians. The Indians or the coloured race started to be viewed as a threat to the position of the British. The British were all out to block any move by the Indians that would enhance their status and put the British in jeopardy.

There was to a great extent a kind of curiosity among the British regarding India and her people. They started to learn about India, the 'Asiatic Society of Bengal' set up by Sir William Jones in the year 1784 was a right place for the English curiosity to be revealed. They even brought out a book named *Asiatic Researchers*. This book contained all the unique things about India. Gradually, it was found that the British connection with India produced writers of prose as well as poetry. Though things in the field of literature started to take shape, the feeling of subjugation, subordination continued. After the colonial period was over, the idea of 'postcolonial' literary theory emerged from the inability expressed by the European theory to deal adequately with the complexities and varied cultural and historical aspects of postcolonial writings (*The Empire Writes Back*). Even the European notion of 'the Universal', theories of style and genre, the assumptions about the global features of language were all radically questioned by the practice of postcolonial writings. The nineteenth century imperial expansion and the culmination of the external, dominating thrust of the Europeans well beyond the boundaries of Europe into the outside world that began during the Renaissance underpinned in complex ways. The imperial forces were so efficient in their imperial expansion that they were able to push consciousness beyond the point at which colonialism would be accepted without question. These colonial forces relegated the postcolonial world to the 'margin'; thus, marginality became an unprecedented source of creative energy. They were able to create a situation of marginalized societies whereby it enabled them to a much commanding position very soon. These notions and ideas are implicit in postcolonial texts from the imperial period to this recent day. Countries once dominated by Britain after gaining independence started to develop their own distinctive style of literature. The first among the different colonized nations was the United States of America. It organised a postcolonial society and this society developed a 'national' literature. The ideas inculcated into this new kind of literature were a part of the optimistic progression to nationhood. It was thought to be the most important and emphatic area in which the difference of national literature from Britain was expressed (Ashcroft, Griffiths and Tiffin, 1989: 15). This American model of writing became an example to follow for all subsequent postcolonial writings. This model highlighted that the postcolonial country's linguistic and cultural traits depend upon its relationship with the colonizing power. The literature that developed in the United States of America was also influenced by the American Revolution, which had forced the question of separate nationality. The American literature as a separate text also began to be accepted. But this literature was accepted as an off-shoot of the 'parent tree'; there evolved many metaphors like 'parent-child', 'stream-tributary', but these acted to keep this new literature in place. This metaphor of past and present stressed age, experience and tradition, and most importantly, the connection between antiquity and value has played a key role in this regard. Though the parent language is considered as the origin and the final authority in question of taste and value, the literature that developed in the United States of America developed different characteristics from Britain. It established the right to be taken as an independent literature. Hence, the concept of national literary difference within English was established. Therefore, the subsequent literature that came up in countries like Nigeria, Australia, and India could be discussed as national creations which are independent rather than being called as the branches of the parent language. This literature evolved thus could be termed as the fundamentals of postcolonial studies, without which perhaps no discourse of the postcolonial could have emerged. The study of the national traditions that existed is the most important aspect of the process of the beginning, as characterised by Nigerian writer Woly Soyinka as the process of self-apprehension (Soyinka, 1976: xi).

VI

Postcolonial elements have been found by critics in many books written in different places around the world. Critics have found many thematic parallels across different literatures in English. The theme of the celebration of the struggle for independence in community and individual emerges in the novels as a device in Raja Rao's *Kanthapura* (India), Ngugi's *A Grain of Wheat* (Kenya), and Reid's *New Day* (Jamaica). In all the novels, we find the theme of the dominating influence of a foreign culture on the life of contemporary postcolonial societies is present in works as diverse as Chinua Achebe's *No Longer at Ease* (Nigeria), George Lamming's *In the Castle of My Skin* (Barbados), (Ashcroft, Griffiths and Tiffin, 2005: 27). Similarly, there are many novels in India that have the postcolonial stress. Novels like that written by O. Chandu Menon named *Indulekha* has the colonial hangover even during the independent era. It was written simply because the author's wife wanted to read a book written in the English fashion of writing. The postcolonial literature always plays an important role in countering the colonial forces. There are many writers of Indian origin whose texts may well be studied from the postcolonial point of view. The writers who have made a prominent place for themselves include names like Salman Rushdie, Vikram Seth, Arundhati Roy and Raja Rao. Among the foreign authors, we have names like E.M. Forster with his *A Passage to India*, and Paul Scott and his *The Jewel in the Crown*. These books have been able to generate a lot of critical response among the readers of postcolonialism. Among the different authors discussed who have written novels in the postcolonial period, Raja Rao's *Kanthapura* published in the year 1938 is a postcolonial novel that captures the psychology and ideology of the Gandhian movement. The trumpet of the freedom struggle had already sounded in the year 1857. This novel *Kanthapura* gives its readers a real insight into the conditions in rural India. The oppression of the rural masses, both by caste hierarchy and the political power structures, was the focal point of the novel. This is a postcolonial text, which came up during the Gandhian movement. The novel focuses on the encounters of the two cultures and shows how while countering the imposing culture, the weaker one always tries to redefine and reinterpret its tradition while seeking its own identity. The novel *Kanthapura* is a postcolonial text that questions the very form of the Western novel; it was because Raja Rao has deliberately used oral tradition and violated the standard English usage. This is a statement of resistance and rejection of English, the language of power and superiority. It brings a device to signify the cultural distinctiveness that exists between the two cultures. The novel *Kanthapura* begins as a tale as told by an old woman and the work transforms to be a political narrative. Thus, there are many texts written after the post-Independence era which help recreate the past, take us back to the colonial period and history is recreated as myth.

According to experts like Ashcroft, Griffiths and Tiffin, postcolonial as a term that affects all the cultures affected by the imperial process from the beginning of colonialism to the present day (Jain and Singh, 2000: 113). According to them, postcolonialism does not mean the period after Independence or after the colonial period, but the term refers to have its beginning from the very first moment of colonial contact. Though the encounter with the British began much earlier, the process of colonization began only after the East India Company started its expansion in India. The revolt of 1857 was an eye-opener for the British as it marked a significant turn of events against the colonizers.

The novels to be discussed include Salman Rushdie's *Midnight's Children,* Vikram Seth's *A Suitable Boy,* and Arundhati Roy's *The God of Small Things.* These texts are quite similar as regards interpretation of reality from a postcolonial point of view. However, sharp differences can also be discerned in their writings in terms of the narrative techniques, linguistic devices and stylistic tendencies. All three novels are written in the postcolonial period with a colonial background. The British hangover still continues in all these novels, which shall be dealt with in the subsequent chapters.

VII

Any work of art needs a kind of subject matter, or some kind of material. Every country for that matter could be a material for fiction writing and it has been purposely selected keeping in view many things about India which have fascinated people since ages.

For example, the cultural diversity, the language and the vibrant life form found in this part of the globe is something unique. Writers before and after the colonial wave setting into this land have always viewed it with a difference. But it was only after the colonization of India that the authors started taking more interest in this country. It was after the coming of the colonizers that there was a complete mystification of life, and a total makeover of the very ethos of life of the Indians. All literature written during the colonial period was termed colonial literature, literature that was suitable to the colonizers. But after the colonial period, things in the Indian panorama witnessed a complete change. The Empire that was trampled had by now become competent enough to write back. India during the colonial period was the centre-stage of all activities. It had always fascinated people, confused and puzzled many in respect of its divergent ways of life and existence. India has always been the land of mysteries, many of which are yet to be explored.

India, the land of diversities, has been the subject of prose fiction written by Indian as well as foreign authors. The wide canvas of ethnicity, colour and the different texture of life adds to the writing of fiction. This very texture has attracted many authors, inspired them and provided a ground to nurture their writing skills to bring out something extraordinary. Many kinds of symbols, from well-known stories, were enlisted by Europeans in their attempt to make sense of strange and complex worlds beyond the seas. India for them is a kind of land beyond the seas, and many stories about strange happenings floated by the travellers who went back with different kinds of experiences. These experiences were true to some extent and mythical as well, but in any case they provided material for prose fiction. The writers like Rudyard Kipling, Edward Thompson, L.H. Myers, E.M. Forster, Paul Scott and Ferrell wrote quite distinctly on materials relating to India. All that these authors wrote was the British response to the experience of India, both real and imaginative or mythical. India is also viewed as a land of romance, adventure and fiction of every sort. The book titled *The British Image of India* by Allen J. Greenberger claims that those images reflected the British impression about India. British imperialism dominated over India for more than two hundred years. Although the Britishers came to rule over this country, they had very little knowledge about this country. All the knowledge that they gathered was from fictions written on this country. The readers of the colonial period and after that were flooded with writings on the Indian subjects in fiction. Many of the writers who contributed to the subject had spent many years studying this Eastern country, but an author like E.M. Forster was a major contributor towards writing of fiction though he had spent only a short period of time in India. All these authors wrote on what they saw in India. Their writings were influenced by the British attitude towards India, also their likes and dislikes of the society in which they moved. When we go into the chronology of facts of literary studies of the vast expanse of the Anglo-Indian fiction, we find that it has opened new routes for all kinds of interactions, such as the attitude of the authors reflected in their novels about the changing attitude to British imperialism in India. Historically, it also represents the length and time in which the British Empire began to disintegrate from a great commanding position and a perceptible empire to record something in the pages of history.

VIII

Keeping in view this changing attitude towards British imperialism, Allen J. Greenberger has divided the whole gamut of Anglo-Indian fiction into three phases. The authors were put into the 'Era of Confidence', the 'Era of Doubt' and the 'Era of Melancholy'. The 'Era of Confidence' extended from 1880–1910, the 'Era of Doubt' from 1910–1935, and the 'Era of Melancholy' from 1935–1960. The writers who fall into different categories exhibited different kinds of attitude towards their subject of India. The authors of the 'Era of Confidence' exhibited their full confidence and faith in the British Empire. For them, the British had reached the zenith of civilization and it is a kind of divine responsibility given to them to rule over the countries populated by the lower races. According to Kipling, British imperialism is an unchallenged and unchangeable truth. It is something of an eternal truth of British life in India. Edward Said rightly argued in his book *Orientalism* that when it comes to British rule, the English are truly a superior class of people. Kipling was also conscious of this fact and deemed such superiority as one of the prime reasons for the English to be the rulers of India. It was a different scenario altogether after the Mutiny of 1857. Nationalism was well organized thereafter. Indian fiction entered a new phase which Greenberger calls the 'Era of Doubt'. The writings of this period began to question the permanence of the British Empire. For the authors who wrote during the 'Era of Confidence', this was an Era of Scepticism. The very confidence in the British Empire was questioned by authors. The confidence that had built up over the years in the Western civilization and felt by the Victorians was followed by doubt. This doubt was on the basis of the *British Image of India from* 1910–1935 (p. 35). As regards the writings on India, the writers opposed to the Raj always attacked the Raj, not basically for what the Raj did to the Indians, but because of what the situation of forcibly ruling over aliens was doing to the British (p. 84). The writers have been placed in different sections by Allen J. Greenberger. A writer like Rudyard Kipling was placed in the 'Era of Confidence', E.M. Forster was put in the 'Era of Doubt', and Paul Scott of *The Jewel in the Crown* was placed in the third category of the 'Era of Melancholy'. According to M. Bryn Davis, all the novels of different authors, in which the images of India appear, were sourced on either army officers or civil servants, who had very little intimacy with the common people and life in India. They had very little or limited idea as their professional creed compelled them to remain aloof from the general masses.

Though different writers were placed in different categories, the images created by them had some grip on the reality. These images and experiences of the British and of Britain rather than India and the Indians do correspond in a broader sense to the development of the British attitudes, not only to India but most of the outside world. The British always patronised the implications of intrinsic racial superiority and this was also quite evident from the writings of the period. The feelings were either expressly or latently present in the works of Rudyard Kipling.

Rudyard Kipling as a child as well as an adult had a varied experience and this was most significant to influence his art. Kipling was so much influenced by India that he carried India into much of his works. He mainly wrote on the stories told to him in his childhood by the Catholic nurse and the Hindu bearer. For all the works of Rudyard Kipling, he is surely a great contributor to the art form of short story. The British also thought by conviction that they have a legitimate right to rule, and they can rule much better, even better than the Indians themselves. This was reflected in all the writings of the period; especially in the 'Era of Confidence'. Kipling as we know is the representative of the 'Era of Confidence', and he as a writer earnestly wanted to project the British attitude, and their views about India. He has done much in this regard through his writings. It was in the year 1872 that Disraeli announced the three most important objectives of the Conservative Party. They were the maintenance of the English institutions all over the world, the preservation of the British Empire and social reforms. But the British in India were shaken from within by the mutiny of 1857, and after the tremor was over, they again settled down to the business of ruling the country. It was during the East-India Company rule that they were able to carry out many developmental works and build up a confidence among the people. Hence, the first period as stated by Allen J. Greenberger was the 'Era of Confidence'. During the time of Kipling, it was certain to inspire a thought of permanence of the British Empire. Kipling in all his writings explicitly approved of the British in India, and he propagated in all his works the myth of the justification of the British rule in India. It is observed by critics that there is a direct link between colonization and travel writings of the period which are explanatory, patronizing and to an extent subversive, as the traveller saw only what they (generally the traveller is a European male) wanted to see (Panwar, 2000: 17). There was a systematizing of nature in the second half of the century; it was in a way trying to assert in a more powerful way the authority of print, and also of the class that controlled it. Kipling had an obsession with cleanliness that he found lacking with the Indians. The law and order which Kipling believed to have been brought by the British to India in a way changed his colonial outlook. David Spurr writes:

'Kipling's gaze identifies itself closely with the force and contempt of colonial authority, exposing the corruption of native Calcutta life when left to its own devices and finding a spatial metaphor for that life in the image of the deceptive, entrapping mazes. The searching, controlling gaze of the police is Kipling's as well. The metaphor of predatory violence underwrites the power of that gaze, while it reveals the duplicity of those who are its object' (ibid.). Kipling somehow had a close relationship with India in spite of his colonial perspective, which is quite evident from his works. Kipling's view about India was stimulated by his nostalgic feelings about India much after he left this country and this is quite expressed in his fictions. Kipling falls into the 'Era of Confidence' as placed by Allen J. Greenberger in his book *British Image of India*; he has been able to link the colonial era at its zenith of glory with its aftermath that followed which was tainted with the Indian freedom struggle. Kipling had a kind of romantic appraisal of India, while E.M. Forster was more ironic, with strains of disenchanted Orientalism. Kipling was a different stuff; he had developed a love of the country as he says, 'I have lived the voices of night-winds through palm leaves, and the song of tree-frogs.' The time when Kipling was writing was when the British were quite firmly based in India; hence, in whatever he wrote, there he displayed his full confidence in them.

The writings of Kipling juxtaposed fiction with his travel writings, which revealed his mind.

'India as always gave Kipling a ground for his creativity, this creativity of Kipling proved to be somewhat outstanding in tradition and his creative writing about India' (ibid., p. 50). Kipling always maintained a dominant stance which is often from a vantage point of a Western eye, which is stereotype, categorizes and universalizes the absolute knowledge about the Orient and the Orientals. Kipling had a different perspective about India, he saw India from within, he could visualize the true Indian colour and develop characters like Lispeth, the hill girl from Kotgarh, and many more colourful characters like little Tod and the most striking of all, Kim. But the general mode of his discourse was colonial. Nicholas Thomas rightly says:

> 'Colonialism is not best understood primarily as a political or economic relationship that is legitimized or justified through ideologies of racism or progress. Rather, colonialism has always, equally importantly and deeply, been a cultural process; its discoveries and trespasses are imagined and energized through signs, metaphors and narratives; even what would seem its purest moments of profit and violence have been mediated and enframed by structures of meaning. Colonial cultures are not simply ideologies that mask, mystify or rationalize forms of oppression that are external to them, they are also expressive and constitutive of colonial relationships in themselves.' (ibid., p. 51)

These are his own personal experiences in and around Shimla, a society in which he was deeply associated throughout his stay in India. Kipling's novel *Three and- an Extra* recreates the society that Kipling was a part of during his stay in India, it also at the same time hints at the anxieties and fears of the English in India which they constantly experienced as an inevitable part of the colonial encounter and consequently in their personal and social responses to one another. Kipling's fictions were a proper representation of his experiences and the life of both the colonized and the colonizers.

Kipling's another story is 'Moti Guj', which is about man-animal relationship. This is about the beast desired by the Indian Kings. Last but not least, *Kim* is Kipling's most successful novel. According to Edward Said, *Kim* is Kipling's only successful long novel which can be read as a mature fiction. This novel also has an Indian base with a colonial perspective and background. Kim was born in Bombay in 1882, again the same setting in case of Salman Rushdie, where his chief protagonist Saleem Sinai was born in 1947, at the stroke of midnight. As discussed by critics like Nicholas Thomas, Kipling's discourse was colonial. *Kim* was a novel that falls in the Era of Confidence. The opening lines of the novel introduce his chief protagonist Kim to the reader as 'He sat in defiance of municipal orders, astride the gun Zam Zammah on his brick platform opposite the 'ajaibgarh' (*Kim*, p. 1); this suggests that authority symbolized by the gun and cultural heritage which the 'ajaibgarh' or the museum stands for and Kim's power over both' (Panwar, 2000: 61). 'In the novel *Kim*, Kipling symbolises the coming together of the Orientals and the Occidentals in the form of John Lockwood Kipling meeting the Lama', which also signifies something much more, that is the East represented by the Lama is a tawny figure and a real seasoned intellectual as regards spirituality. Kipling has an expose of the Indian subcontinent in all regards through his experiences as a travel writer. Kipling in his book has written about the times when the colonial forces had already settled themselves. Rudyard Kipling's *Kim* articulates the hegemonic relationship between the colonizers and the colonized during the British imperial rule in India. In this novel, we find Kipling trying to bring about the difference between the whites and non-whites in India. According to Kipling, 'India was destined to be ruled by a superior class' (Nandi Bhatia) of white men. It is also true that it was the white men's attitude to rule the dark, inferior, downtrodden face of India. Kipling has created a character Hari Babu who is subordinate to Kim. Kipling constructs Hari Babu keeping in view the principle of 'Self', and its 'Other'. He has tried to maintain a binary between the ruler and the ruled (India). Kipling's *Kim* belongs to a class of rulers and Hari Babu is made to occupy the position of the 'Other'. Both Kim and Hari Babu are the products of a colonial upbringing in a colonized society (Kipling's Burden: Representing Colonial authority and constructing the 'other' through Kimball Ohara) India represented by Hari Babu, who is subordinate to Kim. Although Kim is an orphan, yet he has an upper hand over colonial Indian because of his racial heritage. He becomes a sahib by virtue of what Derridean deconstructive reading says 'ceaselessly shutting out this 'other' or opposite, defining himself' in antithesis to it. As for Kipling's imperialist ideology, it is a narrative strategy to represent Kim's authority over the native Inhabitants of the colony (Nandi Bhatia). So, the subject of fiction writing has been a dominant factor by the colonial powers.

Edward Thomson (1886–1946) was a minor novelist, during whose period the confidence that was built up was replaced by doubt and scepticism. The assurance was converted to the sense of guilt. This sense of change was evident among the liberals and the educated class and this is highlighted in *An Indian Day* (1927), which depicts the story of the relationship of the principal functionaries, the British and the Indians. The novel *An Indian Day* also has a historic significance, and it is the first to register the new British mood towards India. Thompson was a humanist novelist who had a human touch in all his writings. Although this novel deals with history and geography to some extent, according to Myers, this cannot be termed a historical novel. But it is all about India in an Indian context. Even though this book is in contrast to Kipling's world of soldiers, engineers and colonialists, this novel stresses on the other truths which are much richer ones about India, the length of its past, the depth of its civilization, and the complexities of its religion and culture. There is the significance of its art and court, the intellectuals and spiritual problems with which the most knowledgeable men struggled.

In E.M. Forster's *A Passage to India*, we find a contrast in humanity represented by Mrs Moor and Mr Fielding on the one hand and the Raj on the other. According to Forster, by 'India', one intends to imply the powerful presence of all that is meant by 'India', its physical presence, its spiritual, historical and psychological influences. Forster, while writing *A Passage to India*, brought about completeness in the theme of India that streams into every nook and corner of life. Over and above, it also influences the psychology of both the ruler and the ruled. In his book *A Passage to India*, Forster has tried to delineate the British characters. The ordinary characters have been evaluated to a supernatural status. 'India likes Gods but as a colonial feature the 'Englishman' likes to pose as Gods'. Among all the writers who wrote on India, there were authors who also attacked the 'Raj' as a decaying institution. It was all because of their loss of faith in the theory and practice of the British Indian Empire. They all suspected the existence of a relationship between the British and the Indians. The last period which Greenberger named as the 'Era of Melancholy' can also be called the 'Era of Dissolution'. The authors of the period remained indifferent towards the Empire. They stopped assessing the achievements of the British and also of the profits and loss of the Indians. There was a sense of uncertainty and loss. It was in the later part of the nineteenth century that the British imperialism was at its height and it remained so till the beginning of this century. It was all because of the British intelligentsia which advocated strongly the British rule over alien countries. The time when E.M. Forster wrote his *A Passage to India* is 1924 after leaving India. The time can be assessed sometime between 1912 and 1924. According to Shamsul Islam, *A Passage to India* was the product of Forster's 'two visits to India'. This novel written by Forster in a period which followed immediately the reinforcement of British imperialism in India by the show of power and the glory of the King-Emperor at the Delhi Durbar in 1911. It was in the year 1922 when Forster was writing *A Passage to India*; he had in mind the misdeeds of the British Empire. This gave him scope to speak of the influence it had on the society. He reflected his idea about the Indo-British relations in his novel: 'It had some political influence – it caused people to think of the link between India and Britain and to doubt if the link was altogether of a healthy nature' (Bose, 1990: 39).

It is often discussed that Forster had an anti-imperial stance, but it was not anti-imperialistic but one of doubt, as has been reflected in *A Passage to India.* The English residents of Chandrapore always exhibit a sense of superiority, even though the relationship between the ruler and the ruled is the same, but just for the sake of hierarchy. The Indians or the colonized live in a low-lying area while the colonizers live on high grounds; both the societies of the Indians and the English contrast sharply. The Indian society is monotonous, haphazard and all in disarray, while the English society is just the opposite. According to Forster, even the roads and their angles, intersections symbolize the colonial net the British had thrown over India.

Shamsul Islam writes in his *Chronicles of the Raj* 'that there were many aspects which constantly remind the Indians that they were a conquered lot and the British were their masters, there was yet another aspect of imperial separation; the club which is a symbol of status, which George Orwell described as 'The spiritual citadel, the seat of British power ...'. The English women who came to India also shared the same feelings and thoughts towards the Indians as their menfolk. This attitude has been reflected in the book *Seeta* by Meadows Taylors. This is set in a period just before the Sepoy Mutiny in 1857 and was written in 1877. There was a kind of social hegemony that was exhibited by the white ladies against the Indians to a large extent and this contributed in a considerable way for the widening of the gap between the colonizers and the colonized.

The hope of receiving humane treatment from the British as a reward for the faith and loyalty was murdered in Jallianwala Bagh in 1919. The contemptuous treatment of the Indians outraged public opinion throughout the country. 'It was a turning point in the lives of the Indians; says Grierson. They saw that the working of the British was nowhere close to the ideals spoken by philosophers like Burke. Grierson succinctly explains an important one in *The Imperial Dream*: 'India must be groomed and educated by her foreign rulers for her role as an enlightened and independent nation' (Bose, 1990).

The imperialism practised by the British in India was instrumental in the breach of trust that was once put in the goodness of British rule and it was replaced by doubt. This was reflected throughout the novel by Forster in his novel *A Passage to India*. He wrote all that was visible; the Anglo-Indian relation has always been characterized as one of hatred, master and servant relationship. The Englishmen like posing as gods and this has been noticed many times earlier. There are many examples of this kind of behaviour in *A Passage to India*, which shows that they are far from behaving as gods should.

The Raj Quartet written by Paul Scott is a sequel to all that happened in India during the British rule and this projected the end of British rule in India. This book written by Paul Scott covered a period of five years from the Quit India movement to the preparation of Partition in 1947, after the British rule ended. So there were many authors who wrote about India as they got ample material to cover their canvas with facts, figures and information about this country, which was primarily ruled by native Kings and subsequently passed on to the colonial forces and finally ended with the independence of the country. The subsequent book *The Jewel in the Crown* (1966) focuses on an interracial love affair between Daphne Manners, an Occident, and Hari Kumar, an Oriental, and the repercussions of the rape of Daphne in a fictional city in India on August 9, 1942, the act by which the British Raj feels threatened by the subjects it has dominated. The Orientals have again been subjected to hatred. Hari Babu is arrested and interrogated by the Superintendent of Police, Ronald Merrick.

The presence of the British in India was a divine grace and they were quite proud of this act of changing the world history by their occupation rights. All that happened in India during the colonial period was reflected in the works of the authors of all the three phases demarcated by Allen J. Greenberger's 'Era of Doubt'. In other words, imperialism was in doubt and the most important writer of this phase was E.M. Forster. All the writings of Forster suggested that his stance was not imperialist, but one of doubt. The political developments in India had forced the writers who fell in this category to express a sense of doubt. The doubt expressed by the authors was on the very existence of the Empire.

Literature in all ages is something that acts as a prism through which any writer projects his ideas about the social structure in terms of fiction writing. Literature, therefore, reflects all norms, attitudes and social values. All the writers of Commonwealth countries had to write in such a way so as to expand the consciousness of the people and try to retrieve the lost glory of their country. This Commonwealth literature deals with the literature of those countries that were ruled by the British. The socio-economic influence of colonialism on the life of the people becomes the main theme of these writers. The Commonwealth period also had some critics, who have divided the two movements of colonization. According to them, it was the colonization of the people and the colonization of territory or land, which had two kinds of responses. Colonization was seen in different forms in different places. In Australia and New Zealand, land was colonized for settlement, but in India, the West Indies and Africa, things were different. These countries witnessed the colonization of people and retreating out after their attitudes were not accepted.

The Commonwealth writers always faced a challenge of breaking through the narrow domestic walls and aiming at knowledge which is free. It was the sole duty of these writers to help regain the dignity of the people lost during the colonial rule. 'This Commonwealth writer has to as a rule help his society regain belief in itself and put away the complexes of the years of denigration and self-abasement generated during the colonial rule' (Post-colonial Discourse, Indian and African Fiction, p. 114). The writer has also to formulate a set of values and new frame of references to project his views about the social abuses that had generated during the colonial period. It was a far-flung concept that during the colonial period, the people of the colonized society should act and think in a rational manner according to their own will. They only did what suited best to their rulers. But after the colonial period was over, the society, which was trampled underfoot by the colonial forces, wrote back with much emphasis and stress. They also gave a vent to their subdued emotions and tried in all ways to regain the lost glory and respect; *The Empire Writes Back,* by Bill Ashcroft, Gareth Griffiths and Helen Tiffin. Many of the writers wrote projecting their own country. Salman Rushdie, Vikram Seth and Arundhati Roy wrote keeping in view India as the colonial subject, because India as a country happens to attract authors worldwide with its multifaceted canvas and thus it becomes a perfect material for fiction writing. Khushwant Singh had written *A Train to Pakistan* (1956), post-Independent novel which is more of history than fiction; it is a tense economical novel which is quite thoroughly true to all the events and the people in the story. In this novel, the central experience and the essential meaning are quite firmly contained within a narrative frame, keeping in view India and all that happened before and after Partition.

IX

Among the writers of the postcolonial period, there were also some women writers who brought a renewed life and an extended subject matter to the Indian novel in English. Although the list seems to be quite exhaustive, to name a few, we have writers like Ruth P. Jhabvala, Nayantara Sehgal, Anita Desai, Kamala Markandaya,

Shashi Deshpande and Arundhati Roy. These are the authors who have chosen India as their main subject matter for writing of fiction. The Indian context has been chosen as the theme of their novels. They have gone to the grassroot to find the subject which is purely of this country and relates to the postcolonial context.

Salman Rushdie has written novels like *Grimus* and *Midnight's Children* and there are many more to his credit. In *Midnight's Children*, we find a kind of dramatization of Indian independence with the projection of the most extravagant Muslim Saleem Sinai, born at the stroke of midnight taking India to its independence. The novel is a historical novel and it combines both Mulk Raj Anand and Raja Rao. The novel also includes the metaphysical habit of Raja Rao and the speculative ability and psychological acumen of R.K. Narayan with elements of magic and fantasy of G.V. Dasani. The core of the novel is a composition of the elements of magic and fantasy. Magical effects are used to indict at once the follies of both the Empire and its aftermath. Rushdie is an expert in the use of magic realism as regards India. He has taken India as a 'magic and reality' combined. India has always been considered by many authors as the land of magic, witchcraft, as it contains many different cultures and ethnic diversities. Yet, it is a colossal structure of modernity. India has been considered as the right material for fiction writing for the simplest reason being the land of miracle and reality. Fantasy has been taken by many authors to project a particular theme or anything relating especially to the postcolonial subject. Salman Rushdie has taken fantasy to highlight India. According to him, India is a land of magic and realism, both existing side by side. Magic realism is a formal technique which combines the 'fantastic with the realist'. It is pointed out by critics as one of the points of conjunctions of postmodernism and postcolonialism (Hutcheon, p. 131). She traces the origin of magic realism as a literary style of Latin America and the Third World countries. According to Linda Hutcheon, 'The postmodern is linked by magic realism to postcolonial literatures that are also negotiating the same tyrannical height of colonial history in conjunction with the past' (ibid., p. 131).

Ania Loomba has described 'postcolonialism' as a loose term. According to her, the prefix 'post' implies an aftermath in two senses – temporal and ideological. Loomba's definition of the term can be applied to Rushdie's text. However, Loomba's definition as regards India also raises questions because when it comes to Rushdie's use of cinema (fantasy) in relation to magic realism, we find India's culture moulded by indigenous fiction and those of the West. This fantasy or so called element of fantasy (cinema) is a Western concept. Magic realism as Linda Hutcheon writes keeping in view Salman Rushdie's *Midnight's Children* and India in particular is a device binding Indian culture of the past to the contemporary multicultural interface. It can also be said that it is only India that the sense of miracle is found in all walks of life. Fantasy and magic have become a part of human life. India, therefore, has become the ground as well as the material for many authors for fiction writing.

India was visited by people from many parts of the globe. These people carried many kinds of images with them to their native countries. The English visitors particularly had many different kinds of images about India. There are two ways of investigating the truth about these images that had built up in the British minds. 'The first explores the principal sources of knowledge and of the influences that helped shape the English way of thinking about India'. 'The second area of investigation confirms to the arrival of the first Englishman in the year 1579, and that came to an end in the year 1618'. India in her long history has been instrumental in affecting people in many diverse ways. India has always been a land of mystery and wonder and for some others, it has been a possibility of immense pelf and power which can be achieved through the conquest of the subcontinent. India as a country has been very keenly observed, criticised and also at times quite irrationally denigrated by authors worldwide. But, for the Indians, India has been a land par excellence. India has been projected in many novels by many writers, both Indian as well as foreign. Western travellers to India, who had in them a literary imagination, have always been puzzled by their Indian experience. The Englishmen who travelled to and from this country carried with them many tales, which were of interest to students. The first Englishman to have visited India was Thomas Stephens, a Jesuit priest, way back in the sixteenth century, to be more precise in the year 1579. Thomas Stephens was the man who learnt Konkani and wrote two poems in Marathi as well. He visited India much before the process of colonization actually began. Thomas Stephens was followed by many more travellers who published memoirs about their experiences when they went back to England. They recorded their impressions of the country and the people and the travel writing made for interesting literature.

Three authors, Rudyard Kipling, E.M. Forster and V.S. Naipaul, have also put down their experiences which were published as an interesting literary genre. People from outside India were so interested in the customs and culture of this country that an author like Murray wrote *A Popular Account of the Manners and Customs of India* (1847). Though the colonization process began much later, the colonial stance was present in this country much earlier. This colonial stance became more pronounced and prominent in the latter half of the nineteenth century.

The colonizers had a mixed feeling about India. George Otto Trevelyan wrote that 'before the coming of the Europeans, there was total disarray in the country'. But, General Slemon writes 'that this is a country where we find that the Europeans (strangers) are safe in the midst of strangers (natives) even in the congregation of a hundred thousand men'. But overall there was a dominant mode of discourse of the period and that was colonial. The term 'colonial discourse' was very frequently used in the book which takes a working definition from Homi Bhabha. According to Homi Bhabha:

> 'Colonial discourse ... is an apparatus that turns on the recognition and disavowal of racial/cultural/historical differences. Its predominant strategic function is the creation of a space for 'subject peoples' through the production of knowledge in terms of which surveillance is exercised and a complex form of pleasure/unpleasure is incited ... . The objective of colonial discourse is to construe with colonized as a population of degenerate types on the basis of racial origins, in order to justify

> conquests and to establish system of administration and instruction' (Panwar, 2000: 16).

In this piece of writing, we find historical facts juxtaposed with fiction. It's a perfect blending of facts and fiction, the riots and the real. The historical and political scenes are all factual. The treatment of prisoners is imaginary, but is based on fact. This novel *The Raj Quartet* is a historical novel concerned with the legacy of the past, race and class discrimination, and conflicting nationalism and ideologies, all in the Indian context. This novel is the historical subject, specific to the failure of the British imperialism, and the turmoil the British created and how they were caught on the wrong foot. The novel also brings forth the partition of India and Pakistan (1947). Though panoramic in scope and microscopic in details, the book recreates events, sights, sounds and smells of British India in the 1940s. This book takes the readers through an exhaustive journey through a metaphysical quest of a resolution between the conflicting forces of love and death, a journey into the mind investigating psychological defences. The journey through which the reader is taken is interrelated with complex unifying effects. England and India, Whites and Black (colour), Soul and Body bad division and insularity are what finally remain of shattered political, sociological and psychological ideals (Weinbaum plot synopsis of the 4th novel in Scott's *The Raj Quartet* and Scott's 5th novel *Staying On,* pp. 94–95). Many writers followed the same subject of India as a colonized nation and that the colonizers were the real masters. The Indians needed to be ruled in order to be more sophisticated and develop as a nation of civilized people.

2 Allegory of History

Rushdie's *Midnight's Children*

Salman Rushdie's second novel appeared under the title *Midnight's Children* in 1981, which is largely considered as a postcolonial text that deals with the ideas of 'nation' and 'history'. Nations are invented and defined as 'imagined community', which have gained currency after the publication of the works of Anderson, and Eric Hobsbawn. Rushdie treats the concept of nation which is fictionalised and projected imaginatively. The text may be viewed as an allegory of Indian history, which enables us to conceive of the image of India as a nation. The chapters of the novel present and depict the postcolonial history which corresponds to one of the twenty-six pickle jars. In this sense, the text is visualised as a chutnification of history. The text intertwines the life of Saleem Sinai, the narrator protagonist, with the development of India after the British rule. He was born at the stroke of midnight as India gained independence. His destiny was tied up with that of India, and to a lesser extent of Pakistan and Bangladesh. The critical attention paid to such migrant authors like Rushdie has given rise to new modes of interpretation of literature written by inhabitants of the former colonies of the British Empire. It involves the area of studies known as postcolonialism, which has paved new approaches, as to how we might interpret literature that is written cross-culturally. Rushdie makes use of colonial metaphors relating to migration, hybridity and the problem of identity.

Ania Loomba's definition of postcolonialism states that the prefix 'post' complicates matters because it implies an 'aftermath' in two senses – temporal, as in coming after, and ideological, as in supplanting. It is the second implication, which critics of the term found contestable: if the inequities of colonial rule have not been erased, it is perhaps premature to proclaim the demise of colonialism. A country may be both postcolonial (in the sense of being formally independent) and neo-colonial (in the sense of remaining economically and or culturally dependent) at the same time (Loomba, 1998: 7) is applicable to Rushdie's novel *Midnight's Children*. Because the main body of the narrative occurs after India becomes independent. The postcolonial literature negotiates the tyrannical burden of colonial history with the past. In *Midnight's Children*, the narrative comprises and compresses Indian cultural history.

Once upon a time, there were Radha and Krishna, and Rama and Sita, and Laila and Majnu also because we are not unaffected by the West, Romeo and Juliet, and Spencer Tracy and Katherine Hepburn. So the characters from the Indian cultural history are intertwined with the characters from the western culture. According to Linda Hutcheon, this is a characteristic of postcolonial and postmodern literature. This is a kind of fusion of the indigenous and non-indigenous cultures, which has a remarkable effect on the Indian mind in the light of Indian independence. The device is that the Indian culture, religion and storytelling and western drama and cinema are resented in *Midnight's Children* in a cohesive manner. It is in this sense that Ania Loomba's theory establishes that *Midnight's Children* is a postcolonial text through its presentation and examination of the temporal and cultured status of India as an independent nation. According to Edward Said, this has been initiated in the text to portray 'the conscious effort to enter into the discourse of Europe and the West, to mix with it, to transform it, to make it acknowledge marginalized or suppressed or forgotten histories … . This is of interest in Rushdie's work' (Said, 1993: 260).

The postcolonial approach to the reading of Rushdie's *Midnight's Children* is, therefore, based on certain fundamental assumptions, which are dealt with by Peter Barry in his book *Beginning Theory*, which is an introduction to literary and cultural theory. In Peter Barry's opinion, 'postcolonial writers create or evoke a postcolonial version of their own nation, rejecting the modern and the contemporary, which is tainted with the colonial status of their countries' (2008: 194). In his view, this is the first characteristic of postcolonial criticism and this may be summed up as 'an awareness of representations of the non-European as exotic or immoral 'Other' (*Beginning Theory*, p. 194). He also states that some postcolonial writers think that the colonizers' language is tainted. To write in this language involves the colonial structure. In this sense, the second characteristic of postcolonial criticism involves this concern with language. He also suggests that the conflicts of the past with the present, of history with modernity that gives rise to a kind of double or hybrid identity, are brought about by the postcolonial situation. This notion of double or fluid identity is the third characteristic of postcolonial writing. This leads to the emphasis on 'cross-cultural' interactions, which may be regarded as the fourth characteristic of postcolonial criticism.

II

The analysis of Rushdie's *Midnight's Children* may be attempted on the basis of these fundamental assumptions. For example, Saleem Sinai's return to India's mythological past and his confusion at the sight of the present political scenario is a typical characteristic of a postcolonial text. Similarly, the consciousness of the dual being in the form of Saleem and Shiva gives rise to the concept of a divided identity. The conflict – Nehru's concept of India as a democratic, secular nation with a fragmented India with its chaotic conditions during Mrs Gandhi's proclamation of Emergency is also another characteristic of a postcolonial text. Saleem Sinai, the protagonist and the narrator, describes the political history of India which runs parallel to his own life story. His physical importance and deformed shape correspond to the chaotic political scenario of postcolonial

India. The narrator Saleem Sinai in a nostalgic mode describes the way how this ancient city was colonized by various invaders beginning with the Portuguese to the British, and now they were about to leave the country in August, 1947. In this novel, reporting of the events was very methodically done by the narrator. He covered all the events which led to the simultaneous birth of the nation (India) and its body (Saleem), that which took place between 13 August and 15th, and they were presented very colourfully. A mixed feeling of both happiness and tension, with each passing moment, was beautifully presented. The public drama that followed was the display of the astrologer's prediction to the top brass of the Congress party, the massacre of Jallianwala Bagh, as also the communal violence and the peace march in Bengal by the Mahatma. This was followed by some kind of private rituals of Amina Sinai and Vanita, the wife of Wee Willie Winkie. Vanita, undergoes labour pain in Dr Narlikar's Nursing Home. She got the first jerk when 'hundreds of miles away, M.A. Jinnah announced the midnight birth of a Muslim nation' (*Midnight's Children,* p. 111). The announcement was marked by a bloody riot in the other side of the border which marked the celebrations for the birth of a 'new myth', the myth of the nation that is India. Saleem writes:

> ... a nation which had never previously existed was about to win its freedom, catapulting us into the world which, although it had five thousand years of history ... was nevertheless quite imaginary, into a mythical land, a country which would never exist except by the efforts of a phenomenal collective will – except in a dream we all agreed to dream. (*Midnight's Children,* p. 112)

It is also observed that a few hours, to be precise six hours, before the stroke of midnight, William Methwold finally gave a stamp to the transfer of property to his Indian heirs to leave this country. It was also seen that he had left a scar in the womb of Vanita, who was in pain on a bed of the charity ward. There were sounds of pain and suffering but the final hour of redemption never arrived. This was the precise moment when Amina Sinai also went into pre-destined labour pain inside a cabin in Dr Narlikar's Nursing Home. August being the month of festivals in Bombay, there were celebrations and performance of rituals on the streets as two things coincided together, one was the arrival of Saleem and the other the independence of India. Prime Minister Nehru unfurls the national Tri-colour and makes an impressive speech, dedicates the nation to the people. All things apart, there were other events as well; expecting mothers went into pain, there were Partition riots, fires and also acts of violence. The gradual and phased development of history of independence is slowly replaced by a clear picture or we can say a positive creation that shall represent the varied vision of reality that is different. It was just at the stroke of midnight that the twins were born of Amina and Vanita. But, as luck would have it, Mary Pereira to fulfil her revengeful act committed a 'private revolutionary act' (*Midnight's Children,* p. 117). She switched them over 'giving the poor baby a life of privilege and condemning the rich born child to poverty' (*Midnight's Children,* p. 117). Fate had Saleem born out of poor mother Vanita, but was fortunate to find Amina as his mother and went on to become 'the chosen child of midnight'. He also by virtue of his parentage went on to win the *Times of India* prize and also receive Prime Minister Nehru's letter of congratulation. The actual reality of his birth was that he was the illegitimate child of a departing colonizer and a poor Hindu woman. He can be termed the product of the sexual oppression of the Occidentals upon the Orientals, and this is clearly highlighted by this event where we find Saleem being born of a colonizer having relations with a colonized.

III

Saleem Sinai represents the newly-born postcolonial nation-state. Here, the matter of illegitimacy also informs the birth of a postcolonial country, that which is a producer of time and history. 'In fact, all over the new India, the dream we all shared, children were being born who were only partially the offspring of their parents – the children of midnight were also the children of the time: fathered, you understand, by history' (*Midnight's Children,* p. 118). We find no link of postcolonial children with origin or purity, time is hybrid and so is history. Neither time nor history moves in a straight line, they both take a curved path. The Sinais found out the act of betrayal by Mary Pereira, but were satisfied by the fact that Saleem was the child of illegal sexual relations between two different races. In a sense, it was also observed: 'we all found that it made no difference! I was still their son: they remained my parents. In a kind of collective failure of imagination, we learned that we simply could not think our way out of our past' (*Midnight's Children,* p. 118).

Gradually the story drifts where we find Saleem growing from a small child to adolescence, where there is a feeling of fragmentation or breaking all over. The selfhood of Saleem is a unilinear development of history from the year of birth 1947 to 1965. Over the years, there have been numerous historical events which show the possible cracks and fissures all over the newly-born nation. Those events that left a blot on the Indian canvas are like the killing of the Mahatma, Five Year Plans that were framed by India, clamping of Martial Law in Pakistan in the year 1958, intrusion of the Chinese in 1962, the theft of the sacred relics from Hazratbal Mosque in Srinagar, death of Nehru and finally culminating with the India-Pakistan war in 1965. This particular period traces the fortune of Saleem's parents, their migration to Pakistan and finally their death in the 1965 war.

The ecstasy before independence on 15 August 1947 was gradually fading away, there were reports of rampant corruption all over and the drastic failure of the government to keep up the promise made by Prime Minister Nehru at the midnight hour. Saleem gradually started to disintegrate; this is metaphorically linked with the cracking of India. The story of Saleem's self was quite unpalatable to his imaginary listener Padma. The combining of his broken self with that of the tools of memory is a clear reflection of his fractured vision of history and the nation. This sense of fragmentation was that what he had inherited from his grandfather Adam Aziz. 'Condemned by a perforated sheet to a life of fragments', Saleem comments ...

The finger which Padma points at Saleem accusingly reminds him of the fisherman; Tai with his finger pointing westward adorned the walls of Saleem's bedroom in Buckingham Villa,

Methwold Estate. This finger is a constant reminder of the oriental vision of wholeness in contrast to the fragments; this also affirms the fact that this newly-born nation is perpetually condemned to a life of fragmentation and hence, Saleem in a way is handcuffed to history. This finger is quite symbolic in pointing at the 'special doom' and 'inescapable destiny' that which awaits Saleem, the narrator, as well as the newly-born nation. Both Saleem and the infant nation began their journeys with a sense of optimism and confidence from their birth. Saleem had a different position, that which was ratified by the Prime Minister. Newspapers celebrated me: politicians ratified my position. Jawaharlal Nehru wrote: Dear Baby Saleem, my belated congratulations on the happy accident of your moment of birth! You are the newest bearer of that ancient face of India which is also eternally young. We shall be watching over your life with the closest attention; it will be, in a sense, the mirror of our own (*Midnight's Children,* p. 122).

It was only after getting an assurance about what will be his role in nation building that Saleem returned home. His umbilical cord preserved in a pickle jar, it was then that he embarked on a 'heroic programme of self-enlargement' (*Midnight's Children,* p. 124). The Five Year Plans framed by India can be compared to the huge appetite of Saleem. The figure of Saleem was quite grotesque, deformed; it represented the map of India which was disfigured because of the partition of its geography. Saleem was born with all sorts of magical powers and was favoured by all at Methwold Estate; the other child of midnight Shiva was the son of Wee Willie Winkie. Because of this, his present status is filled with unspeakable rage. Shiva is considered as the mythological God of procreation and destruction; it was only due to the act of Mary Pareira that he was deprived of his birthright and was doomed to a life of absolute poverty.

The focal point of the narrative is Saleem's search for meaning and Shiva's propensity to chaos, Saleem stands for a social order and elitism while Shiva, for violence. These two emphatic characters make up the contradictions of the Indian political system. The commanding position of Saleem had put great influence on the lives of other individuals, including that of his father Ahmad Sinai. 'I lay in my crib and listened; and everything that happened, happened because of me' (*Midnight's Children,* p. 133). Saleem was quite responsible and felt for both public and private lives, he stands poles apart from Shiva, who represents the 'other', the mindless mob, violence and anarchy.

Saleem was a typical character who could hear voices, in a way he had developed the sixth sense and could receive voices just like All India Radio. Although he had the special qualities, he still had to keep it veiled because he was afraid of his parents. He woke up at midnight to tune in to voices which were not sacred but profane. Saleem had the telepathic ability to hear many things and read the minds of others, he could hear the 'inner monologues of all the teeming millions of masses and classes alike' (*Midnight's Children,* p. 168). He also spoke on the war on language that shook Bombay in the year 1956. According to him, language divided the Indians in postcolonial times. It was time for his miraculous power to be at work. 'The voices babbled in everything from Malayalam to Naga dialects, from the purity of Lucknow Urdu to the Southern slurring of Tamil' (*Midnight's Children,* p. 168). The narration of Saleem is now coming closer to reality and the present day events, it is also describing the episodes, and has become fragmentary in nature. The absence of Padma created a kind of chaotic situation, whereby his memory started to play tricks with him. Here one thing can be discerned from the fact that Saleem makes an error in assessing the date of assassination of Mahatma Gandhi and cannot be relied upon. The narration of Saleem is full of confusion and errors.

Saleem in a desperate bid for meaning and purpose tries and rewrites the whole of history, thereby trying to empower the other midnight children. Saleem makes an attempt to rewrite the history of India, a country which is a dream in the true sense, this is the mingling of the facts with fantasy: 'In my India, Gandhi will always die at the wrong time' (*Midnight's Children,* p. 166). Both the infants suffer at the same time of 'confused thinking'. They are both in a state of confusion of other people's lives. Saleem is transformed into something abstract, he retreats into the clock tower and just like time observes all things happening. Gradually, Saleem is seen travelling the length and breadth of the country, coming to terms with its geography, politics and economics. The narrator highlights that the economics and the politics were found to be tainted by exploitation, corruption and bribery and electoral malpractices.

The magical power that Saleem was gifted with was the telepathic power of 'mind hopping'; this gave him the illusion of an artist. It is this power of his that enables him to enter into the minds of a landlord in Uttar Pradesh who ordered his serfs to set on fire all surplus grains. Saleem was found to be gradually gaining over with different kinds of thoughts; he felt as if he was creating the world, all the other bodies were under his command. He has invented a world which has given him a central position, a position of some authority. Saleem, the narrator, had by now developed a kind of hindsight 'born of the instinct of self-preservation' (*Midnight's Children,* p. 175).

The influence of corruption was evident from the fact that the businessmen were quite happy in India after the First Five Year Plan. India going Western was highlighted from the 'pigmentation disorder' of the Indian businessmen turning White (black money being converted to white). White represents the colonial hangover. This also serves as an allegory for the postcolonial history of the nation. In the story, we find that there is no deliberate attempt by the author to establish any kind of link between history of the nation and history of Saleem Sinai, the narrator and chief protagonist. There is a parodic representation of the official history, that which is deconstructed by Rushdie.

In the novel *Midnight's Children,* Rushdie has made a proper blending of the historical facts like India's launching of the Five Year Plans, linguistic division of the nation that have been fictionalised and juxtaposed with fantasy. Indian businessmen changing colour has been satirically described. There is also politicising of the happenings in the family, outside the family, in the life of the newly-born nation; there is a proper display of experiences that have a role to play in the lives of all those who are related to the nation and its history. As the story proceeds, the narrator goes on to give us a journalistic account of all the historical events. To start with, he speaks about the language riots of 1957, the event that followed the recommendation committee report submitted to Nehru in 1955. This report was brought to effect in the year 1956, whereby 'India had been divided anew, into fourteen states and six centrally administered territories. But the boundaries of these states were not formed by rivers, or mountains or any natural features of the terrains; they were instead walls of words' (*Midnight's Children*, p. 189). The recommendations of the committee had some flaws, it overlooked the state of Bombay province, thereby sparking off violent protests and demonstrations all over Maharashtra. The United Maharashtra Party backed Marathi language and put forth their demand for the state of Maharashtra. The Great Gujarat Party demanded creation of a state north of Bombay with Gujarati as the principle language.

The attempt made by Rushdie to project the trouble-torn newly-born nation is highlighted in the subtitle of the novel 'My tenth Birthday'. Saleem's tenth birthday was not smooth; the day also coincides with the tenth birthday of the nation. This day witnessed natural disasters like storms, floods and hailstones just from nowhere. The sequence of events that happened one after the other shook the claims of the Second Five Year Plan.

IV

The story that Saleem narrates about midnight's children is all about India, it's an Indian story of magic mixed with reality which is both pluralistic as well as mythical in nature. The story includes features like motifs and symbols from Hindu, Muslim and Christian religions, further it also undermines very artistically the purest representations of man and world at large. All the thousand and one children born at the stroke of midnight have special powers and miraculous faculties, still many of them failed to survive. It was because of malnutrition, disease and also misfortune. The number of deaths amounted to four hundred and twenty, a number which is linked to fraud, trickery and deception since ages. The year 1957 marked the tenth birthday of the remaining five hundred and eighty one children who lived a life of absolute isolation and ignorance about one another's existence. These midnight children with their magical powers were the metaphor for 'a thousand and one possibilities' (*Midnight's Children,* p. 200), those that were offered by history to the nation and the various other perspectives of looking at things. *Midnight's Children* can be made to represent many things '... they can be seen as the last throw of everything antiquated and retrogressive in our myth-ridden nation ... or as the true hope of freedom' (*Midnight's Children,* p. 200).

These midnight's children were fathered by history, they represented the promise of a new future 'as though ... history arriving at a point of the highest significance and promise, had chosen to sow, in that instant, the seeds of a future which would genuinely differ from anything the world had seen up to that time' (*Midnight's Children,* p. 195).

In the novel *Midnight's Children,* we find there is an attempt by the author to present different versions of reality and truth. Memory can be the only representative of truth. It is the truth of memory that 'selects, eliminates, alters, exaggerates, minimizes ... but in the end ... creates its own reality, its heterogeneous but usually coherent vision of events' (*Midnight's Children,* p. 211). The general election of 1957 was followed by disturbance, especially in Bombay. The government failed to implement the linguistic division of Bombay and this led to riots between the Marathi and Gujarati speakers. The city witnessed a series of explosions in the reservoirs, which led to acute water scarcity and a 'great cat invasion' (*Midnight's Children,* p. 224).

As part of a parody performance by the child narrator of the newly-born nation, he speaks that 'we must think what we are for', he happens to be the leader of the house. The house assembled to discuss various issues starting from collectivism and individualism to science and religion. These matters referred metaphorically to the difference of opinion among the members of parliament of the newly-born nation. The children, those that were born at the midnight hour or to be more specific Saleem, the chief protagonist, felt within the 'painful, engrossing torture of growing up' (*Midnight's*

Children, p. 229) in the newly-born independent nation. Saleem at one point of time discovers that he has been victimised, the very discovery that he is not the true son of his parents tears him apart. He had always posed to be the hero but reality made him the anti-hero with an illegitimate birth. Saleem, the midnight's child and the most gifted child among all the midnight's children, finds that he has no active role in the day-to-day happenings. He was also for a brief period abandoned by his parents. Collected by aunt Pia and uncle Hanif, he finds himself in a small suffocated room at uncle Hanif's house. He was a victim of events and also 'handcuffed to history' at the same time. Saleem has accepted the temporary banishment happily, he sees himself as the Kolynos kid, the kid on the hoarding at Kemp's Corner announcing the merits of Kolynos toothpaste, the child had been squeezing an 'inexhaustible tube' (*Midnight's Children,* p. 240).

Saleem compares himself with an involuntary Kolynos kid who has been 'squeezing crisis and transformations out of a bottomless tube ... on to his metaphorical toothbrush' (*Midnight's Children,* p. 240). In this novel, Saleem has always tried to assert his position. The central position of Saleem has been stamped by Prime Minister Nehru, who in his letter has congratulated his arrival and also identified him with the newly-born nation. 'Your life, which will be in a sense the mirror of our own' (*Midnight's Children,* p. 238). Rushdie has demonstrated how the newly-born nation and Saleem start to show signs of fragmentation after thirty years of existence. Saleem further also understands how the life of a single individual can influence and reflect the life of a nation. The whole narrative of Saleem provides the readers with a pseudo-scientific explanation to the basic question of the identification of the individual and the newly-born nation. Saleem declares: 'I was linked to history both literally and metaphorically, both actively and passively, in what our scientists might term 'modes of connection' composed of dualistically combined configurations of the two pairs of opposite adverbs' (*Midnight's Children,* p. 238). The point at which Saleem was linked to the nation 'actively-literally' was when he jumped into the language riots and influenced the course of history. His association with the nation 'passively-metaphorically' can be established when as a child he embarked upon a programme of self-enlargement and the infant country also underwent a heroic programme of growth. The historical events that affected Saleem and his family are suggestions of his link with the nation 'passively-literally'. He was 'actively-passively' linked with the nation; it was through his fate being entwined with that of the secular democratic country. Gradually, the cracks and fissures all over his body suggested that he was 'passively-metaphorically' connected and that he assumes the central position as a witness and chronicler of all events both past and present.

Saleem, commanding the central position, also acted as 'part of the surrogate son' (*Midnight's Children,* p. 243) to his uncle and aunt Pia. The stay in his uncle's house felt just 'to exist in the hot sticky heart of a Bombay talkie' (*Midnight's Children,* p. 243). Hanif and Pia started to go down in their career in the cinema – it was then that Hanif began to take the 'myth-life' of India as something inferior even though that provided life and a means of sustenance to the Bombay films. Hanif began to write a realistic film on a pickle factory run by women, he very well knew about the destructive effects of myth and fantasy on the mind of the people of the newly-formed nation, the nation which has pledged to uphold the principle of secularism and modernism. The birth of the nation at midnight gave it a chance to evolve itself from the cocoon of 'fabulous antiquity' of Hindu India and experience the light of modernity. It was seen in subsequent years that the vision of the founding fathers gradually faded away, the many-headed monster started to raise its head in the form of regional divide; religious, linguistic and caste loyalties played an upper hand and the country developed cracks – it started to break … .

The narrator is prophetic, author Rushdie speaks – 'In that time of accelerated events and diseased hours, the past of India rose up to confound her present; the new-born secular state was being given an awesome reminder of its fabulous antiquity … so that people were seized by atavistic longings, and forgetting the new myth of freedom reverted to their old ways, their old rationalistic loyalties and prejudices, and body politic began to crack' (*Midnight's Children,* p. 245).

In nation building and the myth about politics, we find that coalition governance, fundamentalism as regards religion and regional intolerance towards the fag end of the twentieth century and subsequently thereafter confirm the failure of authority about the fate of the nation. In other words, we can say that gradually the nation started to fail; the situation made thus that all things tended to fail themselves.

All the children that were born on the midnight of 15 August 1947, and the nation were growing up. They just can't be taken for granted as regards being immune to the vices of their parents; rather' 'the prejudice and world views of adults began to take over their minds' (*Midnight's Children,* p. 254). This impact made the Midnight Children's Conference break up. The initial excitement of all kinds of experiences started to be replaced by boredom and dissension, that in turn helped to widen the cracks. Poison trickled from the adult, matured mind into the infant mind and they were pulled apart. 'I found children from Maharashtra loathing Gujaratis and fair-skinned northerners reviling Dravidian 'blackies'. There were religious rivalries; and class entered our councils (*Midnight's Children,* p. 254). This is how the Midnight Children's Conference was instrumental in fulfilling the statement of Prime Minister Nehru and in reality became 'a mirror of the nation'. They projected what the nation was in the real sense of the term. The Midnight Children's Conference was also a victim of third world nationalism, its 'endless duality of masses and classes, capital and labour, them and us' (*Midnight's Children,* p. 255). This duality of masses and classes, capital and labour persisted, as also the rivalry between Saleem and Shiva. Saleem was idealistic while Shiva was more practical. Shiva was able to grab the moment of victory and thereby leading to the collapse of Midnight Children's Conference. 'There is no third principle; there is only money and poverty, have and lack, right and left, me against the world' (*Midnight's Children,* p. 255). The innocent children's conference did not get manna from heaven but poison from the discord and cynicism from the adult world and the institutions like Lok Sabha.

Saleem was moved into action by the mutual hypocrisy and the grief of his aunt. The sole thing was that he wanted to teach 'a lesson to all unfaithful wives and mothers' (*Midnight's Children,* p. 262). But in Saleem's 'first attempt at rearranging history' (*Midnight's Children,* p. 260), there was a huge scandal. The subsequent events were the murder of the wife seducer; this can be compared to the killing of Ravana, the abductor of Sita, wife of Rama. 'If Rama himself were alive, would we send him to prison for slaying the abductor of Sita?' (*Midnight's Children,* p. 264). Therefore, Saleem's 'vengeful irruption into history' gave rise to a national crisis. The whole country was put to the dilemma of a choice between rule of heroism and rule of law, between its mythical past and the democratic present. But at the end, we find the rule of law prevails and Sabarmati was sent to prison. This judgment is a reminder that, we are governed by the rule of law and that in the course of time, we have travelled a long distance from our mythical past. Mary Pareira made the revelation in the year 1958, eleven years after the birth of Saleem. This confession by Mary forced the Sinai family out of the world invented by Mary. They left Buckingham Villa and it paved the way for Saleem to enter into another exile in Pakistan. Saleem starts his schooling with Zafar, Amina starts to wither by the realisation that Saleem, her son, is not her son. Here, the author has blended fantasy with reality. Saleem could feel the distance in his mother and sister's gentleness to him. In order to forget this feeling of guilt and remorse that existed at the personal level, Saleem got involved in public events. Saleem was witness to the transformation of a parliamentary democracy into a military dictatorship; it was again by a midnight coup. This was well planned in Gen Zulfikar's house. This godly country of Pakistan had a farcical parliamentary democracy which did not go well. There was rampant corruption, devaluation of values in public life, opportunism, etc., were daily events. Saleem went for a dinner party as a relative of Zulfikar and was instrumental in influencing the fate of Pakistan 'actively-metaphorically' (*Midnight's Children,* p. 297). The change imposed was such that on the night of 7 October 1958, Gen Ayub Khan implemented army rule at a dinner party, and all the officers present gave a silent approval. The political condition in Pakistan rapidly changed, there was confusion and chaos. Saleem being actively involved in the arrangement of the paperpots attracted the attention of Zulfikar, and he treated him as his own son. Thus, Saleem was able to get another father for himself. 'Zulfikar became the latest in the line of men who have been willing to call me ... my son' (*Midnight's Children,* p. 290). 'Midnight has many children; the offspring of independence were all human. Violence, corruption, poverty, general chaos, greed and paperpots ... . I had to go into exile to learn that the children of midnight were more varied than I ... had dreamed' (*Midnight's Children,* p. 291). In the meantime, Amina had also left her husband Ahmed Sinai and went for the godly country of Pakistan.

Peace regained in the family, but at the national level, war took over peace. There was a border dispute with China and India had to fight a full war, on 9 October 1962. Saleem convened a meeting of all the midnight's children in the parliament of his brain. The Indian army made an 'all-out effort' (*Midnight's Children,* p. 298) to stop the Chinese, Saleem made a serious attempt to bring about unity among all the children by trying to forget the differences of race, colour or language. Saleem in a way was accused by the other children of 'secrecy, pervariation, highhandedness, egotism' (*Midnight's Children,* p. 298). The ultimate end was that Saleem was defeated by the midnight's children. The Midnight Children's Conference was shattered due to internal strife, it started to show cracks. Shiva was the one whom Saleem had denied all the birth-right, continued to 'influence history to which Saleem was also connected only by virtue of birth at midnight hour'. The Indian forces were defeated by the Chinese; Saleem developed an inflammation of the sinus. The defeat prompted optimistic rhetoric by the leaders against the Chinese.

V

Saleem was a victim of history, now he also became a victim of his name. His title 'Sinai' suggests something of a place of revelation and also it suggests 'the name of the desert of barrenness, infertility, dust, the name of the end' (*Midnight's Children,* p. 305).

The battle with China ended with defeat of India and Nehru's 'Panch Sheel' in poor light. Amina Sinai and Ahmed Sinai sold Buckingham Villa and immigrated to Pakistan in February 1963. Saleem on reaching Pakistan lost his extraordinary ability of telepathy, but gained the strong sense of smell.

Saleem's narrative also includes Pakistan and its part of the family story. India experienced a strong power struggle in the year 1964; this was the year when Grandmother Naseem Aziz arrived in Pakistan. The power struggle arose out of the sudden and untimely death of Prime Minister Nehru. There were people like Morarji Desai and Jagjivan Ram who united to oppose and stop the establishment of a Nehru dynasty. The fragmentation continued, and this fragmentation of reality and his family showed on Saleem who now 'sought out the oblivion of death' (*Midnight's Children,* p. 341). The narrative continues to describe the Indian air raids during the Indo-Pak war of 1965 on major Pakistani cities, destroying one after the other members of Saleem's 'drained, hopeless family' (*Midnight's Children,* p. 342).

Naseem, Pia, Emerald and other members were killed by the Indian bomb; Saleem escaped death but was hit at the back by his mother's flying spittoon that was flung in the air by a blast. This incident made him free from a historical role, thereby enabling him to move back into a state of purity and innocence. At the personal level Saleem also suffered, although he escaped death during the war but gradually lost his hair, his finger, the magical power of telepathy and now he had lost his memory. Gradually, the whole body started to crack and it coincided with the cracking of the nation, the newly-formed nation. Saleem passed from a state of hope and excitement to a premature state of disenchantment. The India-Pakistan conflict of 1965 made Saleem 'orphaned and purified' (*Midnight's Children,* p. 345). The hit of the spittoon at the back made him lose the power of magic and memory. The story now shifts from West Pakistan to East Pakistan; in the history of the subcontinent, the Bangladesh liberation was a witness to 'the biggest migration' (*Midnight's Children,* p. 357) where people left their homes and fled, there was genocide of the worst order in human history. It was in the year 1971 that the two halves of Pakistan were separated, they were glued to each other by means of religion and finally Bangladesh got freedom.

Saleem after migrating to Pakistan had lost his sense of memory but had gained the sense of smell. Hence, he got enlisted into the 'CUTIA' unit (she-dog unit) of the Pakistan army. He had lost the strong memory; he lost his past and also his own identity, his name. Gradually, he grew old, prematurely old, lost his hair, finger and was called 'Buddha', meaning old in Urdu. Here, at this juncture, he can be called to have attained the expression of calm and quietness like the sage Gautama Buddha. Saleem was quite submissive and learnt the art of submission from Buddha and went on to become a true citizen of Pakistan. In the history of Pakistan, 25th of March 1971 is a important day because Mujibur Rahman declared the birth of Bangladesh. The then President of Pakistan Yahya Khan rushed Pakistani troops to silence the rebellion. Sixty thousand troops were sent at midnight.

It was a bitter experience for Saleem, the Buddha, on the streets of Dacca; he was witness to the ghastly act of the Pakistani army. Women were dragged out of houses and raped, even teachers, students, poets, journalists were ill-treated, killed or arrested. This experience was a bit too much for Saleem. Newspaper offices and factories were ransacked; 'soldiers for Allah' (*Midnight's Children,* p. 357) were found involved in criminal acts of violence just to hold ground and keep the land of the pure united. All around can be seen the traces of violence and criminal acts of Pakistani army, there was so to say a total disarray and confusion, chaos prevailed and value systems died a natural death. The troops started to march toward 'the dark heart of madness' (*Midnight's Children,* p. 358). Saleem made a dash with three soldiers on a boat and entered the Sunderbans 'hungry, unslept, exhausted' (*Midnight's Children,* p. 358) only to be engulfed by the ancient rainforest. The narration moves on parallel lines of space and time. Saleem has entered the Sunderbans with three boy-soldiers on a boat only to escape from the battlefield, to his personal safety. He has in a way deserted the Pakistani army. His journey was a journey from the brutal battle-field of East Pakistan deep into 'historyless anonymity' (*Midnight's Children,* p. 360). Saleem's withdrawal into the forest was just like entering hell, or we can say that he has entered into the sub-conscious, that which the rainforest has externalized. In the course of drifting from one place to another, Saleem met Parvati, the-witch, in Dacca, another child of the midnight with special powers.

Saleem along with his friend Shaeed enters stealthily into the city of Dacca on the night of 14 December to see the dastardly acts committed by the Pakistani army. It was in Bangladesh that Saleem met Parvati-the-witch, and fell trap to her sorcery and felt as though the whole world was slipping out of his clutches and also the power of reality. His 'prophesied historical role' (*Midnight's Children,* p. 382) also seemed to fade away. The only thing that he remembered was the silver spittoon that which acted as a link between him and the outside world. Saleem was outraged at the events that followed his birth and that which linked him to the fate of his country. 'Why, alone of all the more five hundred million, should I have to bear the burden of history' (*Midnight's Children,* p. 382). The anger and outrage revived him to a stage of activeness; he was released from the state of numbness. He suddenly finds himself among the magicians in Delhi, with his silver spittoon in hand, the realisation of feeling for things returns to him.

He has a sudden return to India only to discover himself among magicians in Delhi; this return coincides with the return of Mrs Gandhi to power. The astute desire for power and family securing a secure place is politics was quite evident. There was rampant corruption in high offices as well, Mrs Gandhi in order to achieve this even inclined towards astrology and occult powers. The nation was on reverse gear and Nehru's secular democratic legacy got a big jolt.

Saleem was deeply engrossed in fantasy when he was told by Parvati about her meeting Shiva on the streets of Dacca. Shiva was spotted in military uniform marching down the street; this gave Saleem an idea that Shiva was a man of destiny.

Saleem had a genealogical log book, and once he saw a black leather folder marked 'To secret' and also titled 'Project M.C.C'. Here, he makes a sarcastic remark regarding the national policies going backwards

... but while the Indira Sarkar, like her father's administration, consults daily with purveyors of occult lore, while Benarasi saris help to shape the history of India, I must digress into painful, personal recollections because it was at Uncle Mustapha's that I learnt for certain, about the deaths of my family in the war of 1965 (*Midnight's Children,* p. 394). Saleem has been compared to the Buddha who had scarified worldly pleasures for the sake of finding the truth. Saleem also was moving from one place to another, developed a kind of solidarity between the group of magicians and himself, also had a meeting with the slum dwellers who were subjected to poverty and ills of life but who were free from the 'religious and regionalist bigotry' (*Midnight's Children,* p. 399). Picture Singh was the head of the *magicians'* ghetto, he was able to cast a spell over Saleem and thus Saleem was filled with a sense of optimism. Picture Singh was able to give him an alternative vision of things, he introduced Saleem to politics and revealed to him about the corrupt 'black' economy and 'white' economy. Saleem was explained things by giving examples like the photograph of Mrs Gandhi's hairstyle; her hair was white, snow white on one side and black as night on the other.

The head of the slum had an immense love for Parvati-the-witch, even offered Saleem to marry her but Saleem turned down the offer as he was cursed with impotence.

It was by the year 1974 that the people of India were expressing their displeasure at the Indira Gandhi government as it was highly corrupt. Leaders like *Jaya Prakash* Narayan, and Morarji Desai had formed a coalition known as Janata Morcha against the ruling Congress party. In the year 1975, on a cold morning, L.N. Misra, the Railways Minister, was killed; this was also an important event, Shiva dragged and dumped Parvati in the slum. Saleem had disillusionment with the Communist Picture Singh, leader of the *magicians'* ghetto. Realization came to him that his dream of national salvation was 'insubstantial, the maundering of a fool' (*Midnight's Children,* p. 413).

Saleem married Parvati on Republic Day of 1975. She carried Shiva's child, Saleem converted her to Islam because he wanted the child to be born to have a father not his own. The birth of the child coincided with the proclamation of Emergency by Mrs Gandhi at midnight of 25 June 1975. Prime Minister Mrs Gandhi was found guilty of malpractice in the election campaign of 1971 by the Allahabad High Court. Parvati went into labour at 2 am, the pain lasted for thirteen days and so did the political turmoil in the country and right at the stroke of midnight of 25 June 1975, Mrs Gandhi declared Emergency. The event suspended all civil rights. It was that 'precise instant of the birth of the new India' (*Midnight's Children,* p. 419). That Saleem was blessed with a son Adam Sinai. He was born with outstanding features, flapping ears like that of an elephant quite similar to the elephantine nose of his father Saleem. The time of birth mattered, this child of darkness marked the end of the Nehru era and India's arrival at Emergency. This baby did not cry but just like his adoptive father was 'handcuffed to history' (*Midnight's Children,* p. 420).

It was the midnight of 1975 which brought Aadam Sinai to this world, but he was infected with tuberculosis and was not responding to treatment. This disease was 'darkly metaphorical' (*Midnight's Children,* p. 422) and as it was the period of Emergency, the dark period of Indian history, it also stayed on till the end of it. The child born to Saleem Sinai and Parvati was a mute child, this muteness or speechlessness was an indication of the people's fear during the dark clouds of Emergency and the lack of freedom of speech. Saleem and his son Aadam were both 'handcuffed to history', Saleem was a victim of the 'joint tyrannies of family and fate', and Aadam was a victim of Emergency 'fought ferociously, refusing to yield' (*Midnight's Children,* p. 425). It was the dark period of Indian history when Mrs Gandhi declared Emergency, the son of Saleem was born during this period though was stronger and tougher than his father Saleem but showed signs of stunted growth as there was seizure of freedom to do things at will.

The events that happened one after the other like Adam not responding to treatment made Parvati sad. Saleem had to stay away from his wife and the Government of India made changes in the Constitution and provided the Prime Minister with 'absolute powers' (*Midnight's Children,* p. 424), Saleem could with his extraordinary power of smell sense 'the aroma of despotism' (*Midnight's Children,* p. 424) that was found in the Indian politics.

Saleem became worried about his safety and about the safety of the other midnight's children, there were strange things happening all round and all over the nation. There was a different kind of experience altogether. As part of an endeavour to save the government, suspected people were simply vanishing from different places, so also the slums and ghettos. Prime Minister Indira Gandhi was equated with the nation, the slogan 'India is Indira and Indira is India' was heard loud and clear. There was a sense of absolute fear in the mind of people, news, truth and reality were censored. There were elements to make people aware of the fact that they are now powerless; Indira Gandhi was synonymous with 'Bharat Mata'. She was always surrounded by opportunists, and Shiva was also one of them. Shiva went on to become the henchman and 'a warlord of tyranny' (*Midnight's Children,* p. 430) for Mrs Gandhi. The Emergency that was imposed enforced uniformity and conformity, varied opinions and multiplicity of views were suppressed. The midnight's children were a class apart and hence considered a threat to the unitary world view of the dictatorial authority. Saleem was viewed as a rival whose views ran against the authoritarianism of Prime Minister Indira Gandhi.

The events unfolded one after the other in Indian politics accounted for the irony of the birth of the midnight child who was bestowed with the honour by late Prime Minister Jawaharlal Nehru, 'the role of being the mirror of the nation' through the letter which provided Saleem with the central position and by which 'her own, sloganized centrality was denied' (*Midnight's Children,* p. 427). Here, there is a direct reference to Mrs Gandhi, who learnt about the presence and importance of those midnight's children and went all out to destroy them because they posed an opposition to her idea of conformity and consensus. The sole motive behind the declaration of Emergency Saleem could understand was the destruction of these midnight's children. One cold morning was witness to the kind of coldblooded preparation by the government that was displayed by the arrival of a group of volunteers of the Congress party headed by Sanjay Gandhi. They had come for purposes – civic beautification and forced sterilization. The resistance put up by the slum-dwellers spearheaded by Picture Singh was no match for the use of force by Shiva and his men. Parvati was killed and Saleem was seen running away, but was captured and arrested by Shiva, his arch rival, as he was under instruction from the widow because Saleem was the man 'who held the key to the location of every single one of the children of the midnight' (*Midnight's Children,* p. 432).

Saleem after his arrest was taken to Benaras, forced to abandon his midnight siblings, they were also rounded up, brought to the widow and tortured. Saleem 'gave way to his grief' (*Midnight's Children,* p. 434). Prime Minister Indira Gandhi lived in a world of fear, the fear of power being snatched away, therefore these midnight's children posed a serious threat to her supremacy. The next eighteen days saw big changes all round, these midnight's children were taken to secret places and 'vas-and-tubectomised' by doctors and their 'ectomized parts' (*Midnight's Children,* p. 440) were all destroyed and fed to pie dogs. All the children represented the 'one thousand and one marvellous promises of a numinous midnight' that which Saleem understood. 'Who were we? Broken promises' (*Midnight's Children,* p. 439). Situation therefore became such that Emergency was lifted in the middle of January and Mrs Gandhi's Congress party suffered a heavy loss in the next general elections. The Janata Party headed by Morarji Desai took over. In March all those arrested including the midnight's children were released. The experience of Emergency had traumatized Saleem; he was completely disillusioned by the postcolonial politics. Saleem was completely squeezed of all hope and returned to Delhi thinking that the new age which began with the departing of the colonials on the 15th of August 1947 and which had a new beginning amidst new promises by Jawaharlal Nehru came to an end.

The post-Emergency period was also not quiet for the people. Saleem was released from his status of a protagonist and from the central position to a mere victim like millions others. He was in a way isolated to the extreme side. Saleem was also castrated, for which he prematurely became old 'to whom history could do no more' (*Midnight's Children,* p. 477). Saleem's son Aadam demanded his father's attention and that is what forced Saleem to continue to live, after his return from captivity and even though he had no reason to live. The child was speechless and still had a demand so in a way that was a kind of 'mute autocracy' which was an indication that 'he was a member of a second generation of magical children who would grow far tougher than the first' and they would frame their fate 'in the implacable furnaces of their wills' (*Midnight's Children,* p. 447).

The midnight's children without having cared for the events and facts of Emergency that had destroyed all the thousand and one new hopes and promises of the infant nation, these thousand strong-willed children, those that included Adam Sinai, the illegitimate children of Shiva made a representation to Saleem for regeneration. The birth of *Adam* Sinai floated a lot of optimism all round as he was the child of Shiva and Parvati, the most powerful God and Goddess and the mythical cycle of destruction and regeneration. *Adam* Sinai after his birth instantaneously uttered the word 'abracadabra', which symbolizes and indicates the inheritance of Parvati, the supreme mother.

The narrative of Saleem ended with words and pickles, it ends with his impotence and forced disintegration. There was a sharp decline of the hopes and the thousand possibilities of 15 August 1947. Saleem, whose life mirrored the fate of this nation, began to crack at a quick pace. This cracking up of his body was a reason for Saleem to fasten his initiative to recollect and record his experiences. In a way he tried to bring about an order into the chaotic experiences of life through writing and pickling. He quite understood that there is some kind of distortion in the pickling process as there was unreliability regarding his records of history. Still, Saleem was not quite obsessed with purity, 'to pickle is to give immortality'.

Saleem has now reached a stage when he is completely drained out of power, he now watches his countrymen prepare to celebrate the next Independence Day, that which coincides with his thirty-first birthday. At this point of time, he found all round a sense of distrust, despair and total waste of all things.

The myth that was born in the form of a new nation on 15 August 1947 thirty years ago has now faded into memory or we can say history, there is the need for a new myth in the postcolonial India to inspire the people. The task of this inspiration shall be done by the new generation of Shiva and Parvati's illegitimate offsprings. Saleem was never obsessed with purity because his own generation was a cursed generation 'to be both masters and victims of their times ... and ... sucked into the annihilating whirlpool of the multitudes ... to be unable to live or die in peace' (*Midnight's Children,* p. 463).

It is now that the wheel of destruction and regeneration completes one full circle, something that started with the birth of Saleem, the nation and many events that contributed to a varied experience has now completed one full rotation.

VI

In *Midnight's Children* (1981), Salman Rushdie's chief protagonist, his narrator Saleem Sinai, tells us that in 1947, a nation which never existed was about to win its freedom. Or it can be put another way, India was invented – it was not for the first time, nor for the last time but at the time of its independence. Novelists who have written about India have invented India. In *Midnight's Children*, Rushdie has deliberately re-invented India; the 'ancient face' clearly suggests the long history of the country, still it is often called 'eternally young', recognises the fact that India is continually being invented and Saleem is the newest face of India. According to

Veronica Brady, 'India is a psychic as well as a physical fact, personal even before it is political.'

In order to write about India, it is necessary to imagine the landscape of this vast country, because the novelist is inevitably inventing the history of that place as well as a particular period in the history of that place.

There are four novels which began with a detailed description of Indian topography; they are namely *The Siege of Krishnapur* (1973), by J.G. Ferrell, *A Passage to India* (1924), by E.M. Forster, *Bhawani Junction* (1960), by John Masters and Manohar Malgaonkar's *The Princes* (1963). Authors use various kinds of fictional means to reinvent this country. Example can be taken from Ferrell's novel *The Siege of Krishnapur*. Stage is set in Lucknow but soon afterwards the action is transferred to a fictional place named Krishnapur. Similarly, the other novels have the same means of displaying things about India. In John Masters' book *Bhawani Junction*, there is a kind of situation where he has also taken the neighbouring princely state of Krishnapur which namely corresponds to Jhansi. Though none of the places are found in the map, they still are all true places. It is because of the amalgamation of history and fiction, and because there is no sign of truth, no single India and no single Krishnapur, but there is a deep-rooted fact which is embedded in truth.

India has captured the British imagination in such a way that no other part of the Empire ever managed to do so. It was all because of the fact that they found in India a civilization which was as rich in culture and learning as their own. India also provided the nineteenth century a strong link between the English literary traditions and historical fictions, and on the other, the problems of the Empire and the human spirit. India provided the real background to much of the nineteenth century British fiction writers such as William Makepeace Thackeray, and as Patrick Brantlinger points out, domestic novels like Jane Austen's *Sense and Sensibility* (1811), Charlotte Bronte's *Jane Eyre* (1847), where India has been given a proper place, where people come and return from.

Aristotle had also tried to define the difference between history and fiction; this has become hazy and appears to have confirmed the similarities between the two. There was a time (19th) century when these two, history and literature, were considered to be aimed at historical accuracy to such an extent that all the novels of Bulwer were viewed as history rather than fiction. It also happened that the works of Macaulay and Carlyle, though works of history, were termed and revealed themselves as works of fiction. Hence, one thing can be ascertained that both history and fiction have close ties with each other and shall continue to do so. This is quite evident from the reading of various novels by Vikram Seth and Arundhati Roy.

The nineteenth century at the end gave birth to two new phases – Realism and Naturalism, which harpooned the lives of the middle class and the lower strata of the society; it also provided the most ideal subjects for literature. It was in the 1960s and the 70s that historical fiction had a revival after its apparent death for some time. The use of history in fiction was rediscovered; new life was pumped into the sick body of postmodernism. According to Linda Hutcheon, *postmodern* theory has challenged the traditional attempts to explain the separation between history and literature.

India as a country remains in the British imagination even today, even after many years of independence. Evidence can be seen within ten years of the introduction of the Booker Prize, since four of the Booker winning novels J.G. Ferrell's *The Siege of Krishnapur*, Ruth Jhabvala's *Heat and Dust*, Paul Scott's *Staying On*, and Salman Rushdie's *Midnight's Children* – are all set in India. How far India has been successful in capturing the British imagination can be seen from the success of the films like *Gandhi*, *Heat and Dust*, *A Passage to India* and the television film *Staying On*, *The Jewel in the Crown* and *The Far Pavilions*.

India has been very well studied by writers between 1857 and 1947. These novelists have done exhaustive study in their own fields and do not require much critical study or analysis. Allen J. Greenberger's book *The British Image of India* with its sub-title *The Literature of Imperialism 1880–1960* is a truly exhaustive work about the subcontinent. India has inspired the writing of adventure novels, which flourished throughout the second part of the nineteenth century. *Kim* is one of the finest examples of this kind of novel. This novel by Kipling had a tremendous amount of influence on the popular image of India. *Kim* is one of the novels of the nineteenth century that shows India being treated in a more intellectual vein. It is the first British novel and the most important to be inspired by India, which attempts to present a genuine picture of Indian life. Another serious novel of the nineteenth century was E.M. Forster's *A Passage to India,* it uses its setting for the novel. This novel has its reference in Christine Weston's *Indigo* (1944), and Ruth Jhabvalla's *A New Dominion* (1972), and *Heat and Dust* (1975).

Paul Scott was influenced by *A Passage to India,* which was influenced by *Kim*. Kipling's influence on the image of India, the British India had a big impact on Manohar Malgaonkar and his novel *A Bend in the Ganges* (1964). There are many British authors who have projected India in their own way, much prior to India gaining independence. The novels discussed, namely *Kim* and *A Passage to India,* are not historical novels, but have a strong sense of history. It can also be said that these novels project to some extent the history of India, and over the years have become historical documents. While writing any novel, the rate of change of 'ethos or ideology' must be considered. The writer must try and distance himself from his or her subject. It is always seen that good writers of historical fiction are emotionally detached from their subjects. It is also found that good writers find it difficult to detach themselves emotionally. This thing is evident in the case of Salman Rushdie's novel *Midnight's Children,* where he is very much attached to his book, where the author is very much attached to the historical facts that he has put down and in this novel, the past is more recent. However, he has been able to make his readers live through that year when it actually happened. The writer may make his readers realize that what had happened may happen now. In that case, the present history of India is a direct result of historical events, and also in terms of the 'eternal now' of psychological realism. This suggests that human nature never changes, and this is particularly the intention of Rushdie, and of the South American 'magic realists'.

Writers often use historical figures as the central figures in their works of fiction. In that case there is always the danger that the novel will not represent the very atmosphere of the age, but it is very likely that it may present a picture of an individual in that age. It was again found that in order to avoid this, Scott always lets his important figures grow out of the being of the age. He never explains the age from the position in which his representative is placed. Ideally it is thought that the chief protagonist of a novel should be a fictitious character. Within the wider and more conflicting pressures of that period, he seems to be at work. J.G. Ferrell's *The Siege of Krishnapur* has such a character, and so does Salman Rushdie's *Midnight's Children*. Saleem seems to be one of its kinds, a typical of the eccentrics, the marginalised, and the peripheral figures of fictional history. In other words, he is a character who is bound by the history of India, Saleem is bound inexorably to the wheels of history, his whole existence is determined as much by the history of the thirty-two years before his birth and thirty-two years after. This detailed binding of history is only to show that each individual is created by history and they are also in the process of creating history. Saleem was also a product of history of his times, but he is also creating his own history and constructs his own little world when he invents his own India. Saleem also claims that just like his narrative, he is also falling apart, his body is cracked and his past is spilling out of him. The story that he narrates spreads over sixty-three years swinging back and forth between past and present, which is broken by Saleem's interjections. Quite similar to Saleem' India is also fragmented. It is torn apart by Partition, it is divided and two separate nations have come up. According to Saleem Sinai, 'to understand just one life, one has to swallow the whole world' (*Midnight's Children,* p. 109).

Midnight's Children has a narrator hero Saleem Sinai who is obsessed with the intense desire, the Indian desire, in the novel to swallow whole of the country. Noted critic Srivastava sees this desire 'as a specifically Indian urge to encapsulate the whole of reality' (Srivastava, p. 62). This desire is the main reason for Saleem's downfall and so also of India. The novel *Midnight's Children* is taken as a 'postcolonial meta-fiction, a novel about the Third World novels' (Brennan, 1999: 85).

The novel by Rushdie is the most influential postcolonial novel written in English and that which has the capacity to fictionalize all the events of Indian history from the very birth of the nation, and thereby contributing in the construction of the nation.

In the novel *Midnight's Children*, myths, fantasy and orality or oral discourse play a very important role in explaining and projecting the history of the nation. It is very often found in the texts of Rushdie that the narrators are, more often than not, fantastic yet real, so the elements of reality and fantasy are always there. It was the return of Salman Rushdie to India in the late' 70s that triggered the strong desire within him to reclaim his lost past. The time was when the Indians expressed their anguish over the Congress party (after Emergency) for they thought that it was the betrayal of secular democratic ideals. The novel written by Rushdie tries to recreate in a *postmodernist* way the lost democratic ideals, especially of the marginalized section of the society, and by this the postcolonial history is both fictionalized and mythicised.

The chief protagonist of Salman Rushdie, Saleem Sinai, is a special child among the one thousand and one midnight's children and has been endowed with a special magical power. He does not have a regular form; it is somewhat deformed and can be compared with the political map of India. Although the other children have special powers but they can hardly use it. Saleem and Shiva are born with opposing qualities. Saleem is the epitome of creation, he has within him the mythical creator Brahma whereas Shiva is the god of destruction, and they are opposed to each other. *Midnight's Children* was the first literary attempt by Rushdie to recapture Bombay. *Midnight's Children* explores the ways in which history is given meaning through the retelling of individual experiences. History has been made subjective through the views of the chief protagonist

Saleem Sinai, hence history is fragmented at times. Saleem was born at the precise instance of India's independence, therefore his life is inextricably linked to the events of the time – political, national and even religious. His life parallels that of postcolonial India. It is because Saleem was born at the same time as India, he was able to read the minds of the other midnight's children and communicate with them. In the novel, Rushdie in a way is trying to relate through Saleem's generation of 'midnight's children' to the generation of Indians with whom he was born and raised. Because Saleem was born in of postcolonial India, he must piece together the multifarious fragments of his identity just as India must begin anew in rebuilding her identity in the wake of colonialism. (Cathy Miller, 'Salman Rushdie's 'Stereoscopic Vision': Postcolonial Environments in Midnight's Children' (p. 42). Neil Ten Kortenaar (1995), in his article 'Midnight's Children and the Allegory of History', writes that the novel written by Salman Rushdie is widely read as 'a national allegory giving imaginative form to India and its history'. It has been able to become the central text in Indian literature in English: 'it sounds like a continent finding its voice' (*New York Times* in the cover of the Picador paperback).

Timothy Brennan, the postcolonial critic and writer, says that *Midnight's Children* is a cosmopolitan text that exposes the false consciousness of nationalism. Critics like David Birch take the novel 'as having a radically unstable postmodern allegory, a denial of the very possibility of meaning'. As regards postmodern representative, Linda Hutcheon states that 'it affirms only in order to subvert, but subverts in order to affirm'. *Midnight's Children* – explores the notion of the nation having a stable identity and a single history.

Rushdie's narration is not of the nation, but of the nation in its canonical form, as found in encyclopaedias and other such texts. According to David Lipscomb, 'Rushdie had one such text written by Stanley Wolpert.' Wolpert has written a book *A New History of India*, then came Rushdie's *Midnight's Children*. Wolpert's text highlights the history of Indians, the political history, there is also the story of the nation made by the middle class nationalist politicians. It is also a well-defined narrative form with established origins, narrative watersheds, and an agreed upon chronology of significant events. These events helped shape things for midnight's children.

Rushdie's novel *Midnight's Children* can be called a meditation on the textuality of history and in particular, of that official history that constitutes the nation. The life of Saleem Sinai, the chief protagonist of *Midnight's Children*, is just an extended metaphor of the literal narrative of history.

According to Jameson, the metaphors that Salman Rushdie makes use of to figure the wholeness is precisely the metaphors that Salman Rushdie's novel makes literal 'the nation as a human body, history as the detection of an original crime, and historical knowledge as an omniscience that grants access to the thoughts of strangers.' Jameson further states that Rushdie's novel *Midnight's Children* is a complicated layering of the accepted notion that India was born on 15 August 1947. Stanley Wolpert further writes that '[t]he cultural revival had given birth to revolutionary offspring' (*Midnight's Children*, p. 26), that British India was 'severed as though by caesarean sanction to permit the two nations to be born' (*Midnight's Children*, p. 348), that the Republic of India was 'born' on 26 January 1950 (*Midnight's Children*, p. 356), and that out of the ashes of the Bangladesh War, 'the world's eighth largest nation had been born' (*Midnight's Children*, p. 390).

Rushdie had gone a step further than what has been highlighted by Stanley Wolpert, he has added all the necessary equipment and help required during the birth of a child. It was just at the precise time when Mrs Gandhi declared Emergency, that a son was born to Saleem's wife Parvati. Saleem at that very moment declares two events:

> ... when Parvati pushed in the ghetto, J.P. Narayan, Morarji Desai, were also goading Indira Gandhi, while triplets yelled push push push, leaders of the Janata Morcha urged the Police and Army to disobey the legal orders of the disqualified Prime Minister, so in a sense they were forcing Mrs Gandhi to push, and as the night darkened towards the midnight hour, because nothing ever

happens at any other time, triplets began to screech its coming coming coming, and elsewhere the Prime Minister was going to give birth to a child of her own. (*Midnight's Children,* p. 499)

The metaphor of birth can be termed a part of the larger metaphor of the nation termed as a person *that* cannot be separated from the imaginative construction of the nation. Historians and also to some extent politicians who are conscious of making history that shall be recorded speak of growth and maturity of the nation as if the nation were a human child. They also speak of directions, progress and dangers, as though the nation were on a journey, of wounds and memory, desires and fear, as though the nation had a kind of psychology. In the true sense, the nation through the narrative has been personified and thus makes it possible to even call Nehru the father of the nation to speak, as Stanley Wolpert does about 'the legacy of communalism' (Wolpert, 376). The nation was also coming of age, the metaphor invoked by Indira Gandhi at the time when she declared Emergency: 'there comes a time in the life of a nation when hard decisions have to be taken' (qtd in Wolpert, 397). In *Midnight's Children*, the metaphor of the nation personified is absolutely made literal and also comical. If India were a person, it would be in dispute, and its ability to tell its story would be in question.

The initial pages of the novel begins with the image of the bedsheet stained with 'three drops of old, faded redness', that which Saleem carries forward through the 550 pages calling them to be his 'talisman'. The sheet and stains of blood symbolise that the history of this nation was written in blood.

Catherine Crudy writes that *Midnight's Children* is based on the model of the ancient Indian epics the Mahabharata and Ramayana. The novel, with thirty chapters or 'jars' of pickled personal and national history, moves in a meandering path and makes metronomic swings through time and space. The novel is a kind of link between Rushdie's select style of communication and the oral narrative that he wants to reproduce. It is found in the novel that the history of Saleem Sinai is the history of the nation. History plays an important role in the framing of the country or the construction of the nation. The form adopted by Rushdie provided Saleem Sinai with a way of organising his own complex autobiography. He is literally 'handcuffed' to history' (*Midnight's Children*, p. 9) – the circumstances of his own birth making him analogous to the newly emergent independent nation of India. His narrative is therefore two things at the same time, the story of his own life and also a reflection of the life of India. When he begins, he relates a major chunk of his personal and family history before getting on to describe his own birth. In the course of his description, he swings backwards and forward in time between his present standpoint of 1978, back to the events of his father Adam's childhood, down the memory lane to the simultaneous birth of himself and of free India.

Time is another factor in *Midnight's Children*. Time exerts its authority over the protagonist Saleem, both internally and externally (Crudy, p. 28).

Gradually the story starts to roll and we find Padma is the most trusted listener of Saleem. She is the real critic, judge and guide to Saleem and also to free India. Padma though fictitious is all real. Padma acts as the co-creator of Saleem's narrative, all about India and then about himself. Another key feature of the novel is regarding memory; memory plays an important role in the construction of history and the nation. It is termed the formal strength of the novel, though the narrative is disruptive Rushdie strives to make the readers aware of how important memory is in the 'reconstruction' of the text to be a meaningful narrative. Rushdie himself openly declares in his essay 'Errata' or Unreliable Narration his surprise that he himself was not in India during one of the border disputes, but was quite convinced by his memory that this was the case (*Imaginary Homelands*, p. 24). It holds true to Saleem's recollection of India's 1957 elections, because he places them after his tenth birthday and not before. Here we can say that history comes in fragmented narratives. One thing is sure that in *Midnight's Children*, memory plays a key role in the reconstruction of history and the framing of individual identity. The chief protagonist of the novel rightly puts it, 'Morality, and judgement, character, it all starts with memory' (*Midnight's Children*, p. 381).

Rushdie also admits that memory has its importance in reclaiming the past, and it is memory on which the reconstruction really depends. As discussed, memory is very important for recreating history; on one occasion, Saleem's remembered history intersects with the officers' textbook version. The flying spittoon drains Saleem at the end of Book Two and also 'liberates' him from his past by inducing a state of forgetfulness, loss of memory which is quite a big loss. Thereby Saleem loses his identity, because he does not remember who he is, his link with his past that places him in the social and historical context that which outlines his individuality. Here one thing can be ascertained that memory acts as the chain which connects the postcolonial subjects to his/her disrupted history (colonial past).

Salem Sinai at one point of time speaks of the reinforced idea of the imagined community, when he speaks of India as a country dreamed into existence by a 'phenomenal act of collective will' (*Midnight's Children*, p. 112). So, in a way, the nation was constructed by collective will. *Midnight's Children* is much different than *Grimus* or *Shame*. In *Midnight's Children*, Rushdie addresses Indira Gandhi as 'the Black Widow' in a way to locate her both as a historical reality and monstrous fantasy. Saleem in a way becomes a metaphor for India, but Rushdie has made the relationship between Saleem and India in itself a metaphor for the relationship between any human being and his or her world. Saleem has been made into an international figure by Rushdie when Saleem tries to bury his mementos in the globe.

Rushdie's view differs from that of R.K. Narayan or Khushwant Singh, his idea in *Midnight's Children* is macrocosmic. India, due to its size and complexity and the capability of various kinds of myths and culture, is the ideal metaphor for the condition of the individual in history. Unlike the sense of timelessness in the novels like *The Siege of Krishnapur* and *A Passage to India*, there is always a sense of time in *Midnight's Children*, because Rushdie believes in 'Time

Zone'. 'He begins: 'I was born in the city of Bombay … . Once upon a time. No, that won't do, there is no getting away from the date; I was born in Doctor Narlikar's Nursing Home on 15 August 1947. And the time? The time matters, too. Well then; at midnight. No, it's important to be more … . On the stroke of midnight, as a matter of fact. Clock-hands joined palms in respectful greetings as I came. Oh, spell it out, spell it out; at the precise instant of India's independence, I tumbled forth to the world (*Midnight's Children*, p. 9).'

VII

It is quite significant to interpret magic realism in connection with the *postcolonial* discourse, because Rushdie has quite consciously executed magic realism as a stylistic device in this postcolonial text. In fact, the term 'postcolonial' is as problematic as 'magic realism', but, in a general way, postcolonial writing includes a wide range of discursive methods which are not compatible with colonialism and colonial ideologies. Moreover, the concept of identity, history and perspective are of great significance to postcolonial writers. The consequence of colonization process is that the subject people in a colonial system are compelled to be placed in two conflicting worlds or spaces. According to Linda Hutcheon, it is a duality of 'postcolonial doubled identity and history' (Hutcheon, p. 7). The 'reason' and 'logic' of the Western intellectual tradition juxtaposed with the 'mysterious' and 'mythic' perspective of the natives. These two worlds are actually incompatible with each other, but the subjugated people in a colonized State have to question their identity in terms of the dual worlds or spaces which they inhabit.

Canadian critic Robert Wilson refers to these spatial effects of magic realism, which are very relevant in the context of postcolonial writing. In his opinion, magic realism creates 'a space in which the spatial effects of canonical realism and those of axiomatic fantasy are interwoven … in magic realism, space is hybrid (opposing and conflicting properties are co-present)' (p. 8). This phenomenon is described by Wilson as 'dual spatiality'.

Stephen Slemon claims that magic realism encodes 'a concept of resistance to the massive imperial centre and its totalizing system' (p. 18). Magic realism contests the limitations of colonial space by hinting at a 'dual spatiality'. In this context, any idea of a single, unified global view of reality involves the problematic issues. In the opinion of Chanady, it 'allows us to see dimensions of reality of which we are not normally aware' (Chanady, 1985).

According to Linda Hutcheon, the formal technique of magic realism enables the author to bring about the conjunction of *postmodernism* and *postcolonialism*. She traces the origin of magic realism as literary style to Latin American and Third World countries. Such a text negotiates the burden of colonial history with the traits of *postmodernism*. *Midnight's Children* is an example of a postcolonial text, intertwined with the aspects of magic realism. Rushdie employed magic realism to redefine the novel in a postcolonial context. It is by this that technique he projects the postcolonial history in terms of the marginalized voices, the histories of women and the cultural minorities.

India has always been termed by many authors a land of magic, and mystery. In this novel, there is a mingling of fantasy with reality. According to Linda Hutcheon, 'magic realism', which is the characteristic mixing of the fantastic and the realist, is highlighted as one of the points of conjunction of *postmodernism* and also postcolonialism. The *postmodern* is linked to the *postcolonial* literature. Ania Loomba in her book *Defining Colonialism/ Postcolonialism* writes that the word post in postcolonialism is a complex matter because it complicates the word or the prefix 'post' implies an 'aftermath', again in two senses the temporal and the ideological.

The second implication of the term is found by critics to be more contestable. According to them, if the inequities of colonial rule have not been erased, it's quite premature to have declared the demise of colonialism. Loomba's colonialism can be applied to Rushdie's text. In the temporal sense, *Midnight's Children* is postcolonial, as the main body of the narrative occurs after India became independent. The whole narrative of *Midnight's Children* consists of the stories which Saleem Sinai narrates to his wife-to-be Padma.

The most striking feature of Rushdie's novel is realism mixed with fantasy. Magic realism is a device binding culture of the past to the contemporary multicultural interface. It is from the year 1980 that the terms like 'magic' realism, 'magical' realism and 'marvellous' realism have been widely in use. In a way these are kind of oxymorons that describe the forced relationship between irreconcilable terms. The term magic realism for that matter has been addressed differently in different countries. Still there is a confusion that surrounds the term, and that is due to lack of accuracy of its application. As in the case of Germany, the term originated from 'Magischer Realism' which was again translated to Dutch 'Magisch-Realisme' and in English 'Magic Realism'. Although many people had heard of the terms, yet very few are clear about the concept of the terms. 'Magic Realism' is a concept of mystery (that) does not descend to the represented world, but rather hides and palpitates behind it' (Roh, 1995: 15)'. But 'magical realism' as understood in the words of Salman Rushdie is the comingling of the improbable with the mundane (1982: 9). Rushdie's use of magic realism in the text involves the telepathic abilities of Saleem to communicate with the other thousand and one children around him. Prior to Rushdie, the term magic realism was originally applied in the year 1920s by a school of painters; it is also used to describe the works of Jorge Luis Borges in Argentina, as well as in the works of other writers such as Gabriel Garcia Marquez, James Joyce, etc. These writers interweave in an ever-shifting pattern a sharply etched realism, representing events and descriptive details together with fantastic and dreamlike elements, as well as with materials derived from myths and fairy tales. But whatever be the derivation, they are widely used and discussed most frequently as the concept of reality.

It is often a general conception that magical realist writings are to be found confined to a particular location. This is quite misleading, since it is after all a narrative mode or may be a way of thinking in a different perspective; hence these concepts just cannot be confined to one geographical location. But, one thing is for sure of magic realist fictions having a rural background or backdrop. The best example can be had of the Colombian novelist Gabriel

Garcia Marquez, who has set most of his celebrated novel *One Hundred Years of Solitude* in the fictional town of Macondo in the Caribbean coast of Colombia. Salman Rushdie has magic realism as the most important feature of his fiction, but has set his novels in the world's largest urban areas such as London, Bombay or New York and happens to be most notable of these writers. But, though set in an urban backdrop, the novels are portrayed from the marginalized class of people who have been deprived of political power, whatever may be their profession. This is the main reason for magical realism to be associated with fictions that tell the story of those who are on the margins of political power and affluent society. Magical or magic realism although has its domain spread over many countries with many writers having it as the main theme of their works, but the best known writer of magic realism in English is Salman Rushdie. The main theme of writing of postcolonial writers is against the British colonial rule. This is the factor that connects the English language magic realist writers with each other. As for Salman Rushdie, apart from myths and fairy tales, cinema is yet another medium of postcolonial cultural interface used by Rushdie. Cinema plays a very important role in Rushdie's *Midnight's Children*. The cinema is projected by Rushdie in *Midnight's Children* as a postcolonial cultural interface. Rushdie attempts to make use of the setting in which he examines the effects of the interplay of the subtle fantasy within the perceptions of realty. This is moulded by both Hollywood and the Indian film industry. The scattered references of the cinema continually inform the narrator of midnight's children. Rushdie's rickshaw boy Rashid, after leaving the cinema, contemplates in his mind what he has just witnessed, which Rushdie terms an 'Eastern Western'. The production is not only a curious hybrid of Hollywood cowboy film and the Hindu culture, but it is also a signifier of the presence of interconnected Western and Indian influences. All this is within the Indian postcolonial spheres. Cinema renders a postcolonial view of Bollywood production in India. They are representative of a popular Indian medium after independence had been gained, but also intertwined with Hollywood culture. Saleem's perception of himself in his memory and within his fantastic narrative is also shaped by cinema. Here, cinema becomes a further device for others and their perception of themselves. Rushdie feels that cinema plays a very important role in the field of culture. Hence, this medium is quite important as far as the hybrid postcolonial Indian culture is concerned. It is from this medium that a hybrid postcolonial Indian develops.

According to Kum Kum Sangari, because of its inherent mixture of opposing perspectives, magical realist writing is the perfect form of writing for any postcolonial middle class emigrant writer like Rushdie, who has been totally influenced by British colonialism and also Indian popular culture. Salman Rushdie, who is a highly political writer and who is deeply concerned with the future of India, is also fascinated by its diversity, religion, and languages and explains that 'My India has always been based on ideas of multiplicity, pluralism, and hybridity'(Rushdie, 1991: 32). His famed novel *Midnight's Children* (1981–1982) provides the best example of a novel that attempts to provide a kind of modern epic for a country which over the years has moved in leaps and bounds from a confident nation full of promises to a diverse nation which is now conscious of its own failings.

The novel *Midnight's Children* adopts a magic realist device emphasising the continued struggle to come to terms with identity, within the polarity of the postcolonial. These midnight's children by virtue of their birth are children of the times; they are the magical creations, India as a country is termed a myth-ridden nation. Saleem was born at the stroke of midnight on 15 August, the precise moment of India's independence from British rule. Saleem is the son of poor parents, but is switched with another child at birth. Saleem possesses supernatural powers, the most unusual of which is the ability to read other people's thoughts. His life mirrors the development of India as a nation; here, the personal life of Saleem is linked with the history of the nation. Saleem was born at the same time as India when it came into being and is a part of the group of children who were all born at the same time. Saleem always tries to explore his fragmented identity. He is the child of multiple nations, religions, languages, and political parties, he has a conflicted and often contradictory sense of self (*Midnight's Chiidren*, p. 219).

Saleem also claims that just like his narrative, he is also falling apart, his body is cracked and his past is spilling out of him. The story that he narrates spreads over sixty-three years, swinging back and forth between past and present, which is broken by Saleem's interjections. Quite similar to Saleem, India is also fragmented. It is torn apart by Partition, it is divided and two separate nations have come up. Language marchers have also tried to divide the nation further on linguistic lines.

Magic realism is therefore seen as a device binding Indian culture of the past to the contemporary multicultural interface. 'The narratives of displacement' – Rushdie's midnight's children are a typical narrative of displacement (*Reading in English Literature: Nation, Culture and Identity*). There is a sense of nostalgia in Rushdie's essays entitled *Imaginary Homelands*, written in the year 1982. Rushdie brings forth his idea of loss when he returned to Bombay; he proudly stood outside his house after an absence of half of his life, and thought about the losses he had incurred in those years. *Midnight's Children* was born out of the necessity to 'restore his past to himself'. Exiles, imagination and expatriates played an important role in the life of Rushdie and made him feel that he can never reclaim whatever he had lost. A sense of loss pervaded his entire body and soul; he was forced to create fictions – no real cities or villages but invisible ones, *Imaginary Homelands*.

Displacement has always played an important role in the works of Rushdie, in *Midnight's Children* there is a sense of multiple displacements – personal, geographical and physical. It can be said that the novel was born out of the process of one of the displacements that is of the author – that which was caused by imagination. In fact, the theme of place and displacement is recurrent in postcolonial fiction.

Midnight's Children recreates Rushdie's sense of an India of the minds through the novelistic conventions. These are established by Rushdie as a trendsetter for writing postcolonial novels, and in this sense, he seems to have influenced other immigrant writers. *Midnight's Children* celebrates the eclecticism by highlighting thematic focus on national, cultural and personal redefinition. It is also observed that for postcolonial writers, group identity becomes more significant than individual identity. History plays an important role in the construction of group identity.

According to Rushdie, reality is built on our prejudices, misconceptions and ignorance as well as our perceptiveness and knowledge. The reading of Saleem's narrations might be an analogy for our everyday attempt to read the world. Rushdie tries to capture important points of Indian history, he does it with a purpose and in a form that attempts to recapture traditional Indian literary genesis. The novel by Rushdie can be seen as the novel of the immigrant experience and a product of authorial displacement … .

Midnight's Children explores the ways in which history is given meaning through telling of individual experience. The chief protagonist of the novel Saleem was also born at the same time as India when it came into being; he is part of the group of children who were all born at the same time. They were all born with magical gifts. Saleem narrates the story of India in retrospect. He is bestowed with the special ability of magic, and witnesses and also participates in many magical things. He can foresee many things like bodies disappearing, he also finds himself riding through the air with a witch. Most of the things that he says have their origin in magical tales such as *A Thousand and One Nights*, but they are also associated with the Indian circus acts like the 'Indian rope tricks' (Bouers, 2007: 54). Saleem is a typical character who represents both the subject and the object, sometimes simultaneously. He is at the same time one who perceives and also the object that is perceived. At times, he refers to himself as the third person before reverting to the first person narrative. In *Midnight's Children*, identity is constructed through identification, either with religion or with a family. The exchange of babies at birth did crystallize one identity as Saleem and the other as Shiva (*Midnight's Children*, p. 130).

The personal history of Saleem is the history of India; Saleem calls himself a historian and links his own life to the times. Bombay and Karachi are the cities of illusion, of grotesque houses springing madly or shifting foundations. This represents the country of age of Saleem Sinai and that of the whole South Pacific Asia or the entire subcontinent (*Midnight's Children*, p. 132). It was in the Eighties that the element of fantasy came into the writing in English, but this particular thing is quite old for us. The concept of recreating the past with the help of fantasy is quite old; it was a medium to amalgam the realistic with the fantastic. Among the modern writers, Salman Rushdie's *Midnight's Children* is full of fantasy, he has used magic to depict 'reality', in other words it is assumed that 'magic realism' plays a vital role in projecting the dynamism of the postcolonial writers who were able to write against the Raj. The formal technique used is magic realism, according to Linda Hutcheon, is a mingling of the fantastic and the realist. Hutcheon has traced the origin of magic realism as a literary style in Latin America and the Third World countries. It is accompanied by the definition of the postmodern texts that signifies a change from modernism as a historical burden of the past; it is a text that reconstructs the relationship to what comes before, or between the past and present.

The narrative paradigm of *Midnight's Children* consists of a tale which Saleem Sinai recounts orally to his wife-to-be Padma. There is a self-referential narrative written in a single paragraph – Saleem refers to himself in first person: And I, recalls the indigenous Indian culture. There is a cultural similarity with the *Arabian Nights*, based on the oral narration, the events of Rushdie's text also parallel the magical nature of the narrative recounted in the *Arabian Nights* as in Saleem being electrocuted in the latrine or his journey in the invisible basket. The narration of *Midnight's Children* contains and compresses Indian cultural history. The way Saleem addresses – there were Radha and Krishna, Rama and Sita, Laila and Majnu, also Romeo and Juliet, and Spencer Tracy and Katherine Hepburn. Here comes Hutcheon's postmodern perspective; characters of the western culture are intertwined with that of the Indian cultural history; the device that they signify –

Indian culture, religion, and cinema – all these elements are present in Rushdie's text with postcolonial Indian history to examine both the effects of non-indigenous cultures upon the Indian mind and all this keeping in mind the Indian independence.

Ania Loomba's theory on postcolonialism is a malleable definition which can be applied to Rushdie's text. It can be said that in the temporal sense, *Midnight's Children* is postcolonial as the main content of the narration has occurred after India's independence. The use of cinema as magic realism to explain reality by Rushdie has given ample scope for questions regarding Ania Loomba's 'ideological' sense; because the cultural scenario of India is reshaped by indigenous fictions and also that of the West.

The entire narrative paradigm of *Midnight's Children* consists of a tale that comprises his life story ... which Saleem Sinai describes to his wife-to-be Padma. It is a self-referential narrative '(within a simple paragraph, Saleem refers to himself in the first person: 'And I wishing upon myself the curse of Nadir Khan ... .' 'I tell you', Saleem cried, 'It is true ...') recalls indigenous Indian culture, particularly the similarly orally recounted in the *Arabian Nights* (consider the attempts to electrocute Saleem in the latrine (*in Midnight's Children,* p. 353), or his journey in the basket of invisibility' (*Midnight's Children,* p. 383).

According to Edward W. Said, the temporal and cultural status has been contained in the text to project the 'conscious effort to enter into a kind of discourse of Europe and the West, to mix with it, transform it, to make it fit to acknowledge marginalised or suppressed or forgotten histories ... . (This) is of particular interest in Rushdie's work' (*Midnight's Children,* p. 260).

Magic realism as pointed out by Linda Hutcheon is just a style of writing in general, having a special reference to *Midnight's Children*. It is discussed before as a device that binds the Indian culture of the past with that of the multilingual interfaces of the present times. Stephen Slemon opines that in any magic realist text, 'in the language of narration there is a constant tussle between the opposing factors, each working towards the creation of a fictional world.' An example can be had from the world of fantasy and the world of reality, they both struggle to have the reader's attention. In *Midnight's Children,* the fantastic is easily spotted while the realistic makes itself heard.

VIII

'Magic Realist' texts, 'Slemon continues, 'tend to display a preoccupation with images of borders and centres, and to work towards destabilising their fixity' (13). Rushdie has attempted to achieve this in his novel; here it takes place between the borders of the cinematic and the cinema screen; that is the ground which is very carefully examined with regard to the subtle fantasy at play, within the perception of reality. This is reshaped by both Hollywood and Indian film industry.

There are scattered references to the cinema, that which acts as a constant reminder of *Midnight's Children*. There is a perfect blend of hybrid Hollywood cinema and Hindu culture, which acts as a signifier of the presence of the interconnected Western and Indian influences within the postcolonial Indian sphere.

The explanation of the postcolonial presents a kind of view of the 'Bollywood' productions in India; these are the representations of the popular Indian medium after India's independence, but one being entangled with Western 'Hollywood' culture.

Cinema being such a popular medium becomes Rushdie's most important device for magic realism, because films always help transform the very idea of the other and also their perception of themselves. Indian film industry in a way becomes a medium for the possibility of new investigations and construction of Indian cultural identity. According to Edward W. Said, *Midnight's Children* is a 'work based on the liberating imagination of independence itself, with all its anomalies and contradictions working themselves out' (260).

Rushdie has presented the cinematic influence of Indian culture in a comical manner. In his text, there is an objective world of historical events that mould history. Postcolonial Indian culture is a blend of Western and Indian and masks the harsh nature of political and historical events. Cinema has always had a multicultural interface; it is a true representation of life and a combination of the 'Eastern, Western'. As rightly said by Rushdie, 'this medium has represented reality in a true sense and in a better way'. The cinema screen is termed as a ground for examination of the two extreme polarities, 'universalism', the 'notion' of a unitary homogeneous human nature that marginalises and excludes the distinctive characteristics, the difference of postcolonial societies, and the differences which find 'universalism' disappearing into an endless network of provincial and specific determination where even the most apparently 'essential' features of human life become provisional and contingent' (Ashcroft, Griffiths and Tiffin, 1999: 55). This feature is directly implied to Rushdie while writing reality. Events when seen from a distance seem like vague generalisations, but when Saleem moves closer to the cinema screen, from the back seat to the front, Saleem considers that gradually the stars' faces dissolve into dancing grains, tiny details assume grotesque proportions; the illusions dissolve' or rather it becomes clear that the illusion itself is reality. (*Midnight's Children*, p. 166).

'Magic Realism', according to Linda Hutcheon, in *Midnight's Children* is a special device binding Indian culture of the past with that of the contemporary multicultural interface. Rushdie has used this technique in his novel to project reality; reality is a question of perspective; the further one gets from the past, the more concrete and plausible it seems – but as one approaches the present, it inevitably seems more and more incredible. Rushdie has used it in the text that involves telepathy and supernatural abilities of his chief protagonist Saleem Sinai. According to Stephen Slemon, the very language used in a magic realist text has two oppositional systems battering each other. If we take these details to be the world of fantasy and the world of realty, both these factors can be seen to be present and compelling to have the reader's attention. This fantasy is quite easily heard in the *Midnight's Children;* it is through the fantastic that the realistic makes itself heard.

Rushdie has tried to highlight the realistic features through the fantastic – it is through his calculations that we make a rough assessment of the birth of the Indian subcontinent or the thousand-headed monster as he himself described it. This calculation of Rushdie or comment enables the gift of telepathy to be perceived as a magical objective of Indian society which influences the individual psyche. It can be that people live in a society which is intermingled with each other in such a manner that people hardly live alone. This is perhaps not so in Europe. The language of Saleem and his utterances, his telepathy becomes simultaneously a magical and realistic device to signify the polyglot frenzy. This is what consists of the inner monologue of all the teeming millions. Rushdie also tried his hand at another form of magic realist device. Cinema is another postcolonial cultural interface. According to Stephen Slemon, magic realist texts had to display a preoccupation with images of borders, and centres and works towards destabilising their fixity. Salman Rushdie attempts this within the borders of the cinematic and cinema. According to Rushdie, in the cinema screen, there is every scope to examine it perceptively and it is also perceptible. Here, he perceptively examines the effects of the suitable fantasy at play within the framework of reality, moulded by both Hollywood and also Indian film industry. In this novel, there are scattered references of the cinema that act as a constant reminder of *Midnight's Children.* This mode of fantasy is highlighted by Rushdie through Rashid, the rickshaw boy, who has just watched a film which Rushdie ironically termed 'Eastern-Western'. The production that Rushdie talks of is not only a curious hybrid of Hollywood cowboy film and Hindu culture but it is also a signifier of the presence of the interconnected Western and Indian influences within the postcolonial spheres. Cinema is a colonial feature in a postcolonial context, as viewed by Rushdie. It can be discerned that the cinematic rendering of the postcolonial presents a benevolent view of the 'Bollywood Production' of India. Though it is a popular Indian medium after India got independence, still these elements are strongly interwoven with each other; the Western Hollywood culture being the most important and dominant by itself than the Bollywood industry.

Hybridity of cinema has always played an important role in the reshaping of the individuals who are frozen by its magic(al) romance. Saleem's perception of himself in his memory and within his fantastic narrative is also shaped by cinema. Cinema as in the case of Rushdie's *Midnight's Children,* has become a strong device of magic realism. It is an instrument to transform the perception of others and also their perception of others. It is through cinema that people for a brief period are transformed from this mundane world to the world of fantasy, which seems to be quite natural and realistic. This mode of magic realism as observed by critics becomes a window after the attainment of independence by India, for the possibility of new investigations and constructions of the Indian cultural identity.

As Edward Said writes in his book *Orientalism*, *Midnight's Children* is a work on the literary imagination of independence. All the faults and contradictions are continually working themselves out. Rushdie has always presented the cinematic influence of Indian culture; in a joyous manner, but there is also an undercurrent of scepticism. There is always adherence to magical fantastic fictions – whether cinematic, oral, Indian, or Western. He postulates in doing so that there is an objective world of historical events that shape history. In a way, the postcolonial culture, in mingling with the Western as well as Indian historical events, at the end questions the achievements of the 'Complete Indian Identity', that is completely free from time, space and culture and over and above outside influences. It is found that in the simple child-like fantasy, individual identities can be constructed quite easily; examples can be taken of Saleem Sinai. The novel *Midnight's Children* presents a nation, India, in its infancy, which just like Saleem enjoys a fantastic tale and sees the magical as omnipresent. Saleem's story is about the interrelatedness of the personal and the public, and of his own life with the history of modern India. Salman portrayed the history of India with the elements of marvellous and the supernatural, as it helps to resolve the immigrant's dilemma. Rushdie in his essay on Gunter Grass writes, 'I grew upon Warden Road, Bombay, now it is Bhullabhai Desai Road'. Of course the decolonised names tell of a conflict, assertive spirit in the independent state. But, loss of the past attachments remains a loss. What to do? Shrug. And pickle the past books (*Imaginary Homelands,* p. 277).

Rushdie in his work has to make a concoction of all things. Rising from the pages 'comes the unmistakable whiff of chutney' (37) like the flavours of all the ingredients, put many lives, events, miracles, places, rumours-mixed with each other in a dense 'comingling of the improbable and the mundane'(9). It was when an immigrant writer writes about the past, he creates fictions, not actual cities or villages, but invisible ones, imaginary homelands, 'India of the minds' (*Imaginary Homelands,* p. 10). *Midnight's Children* is a similar one, one that describes India's past, history of the nation, the past is juxtaposed with the present, and it is all done with the help of fantasy. This fantasy highlights or projects the realistic; there is an amalgamation of the past and the present. In *Midnight's Children,* Rushdie projects the real India, but his version of India, the India which is a world of fantasy. It is a fantastic India.

Midnight's Children can be well placed between Gunter Grass's *The Tin Drum* and Gabriel Garcia Marquez's *One Hundred Years of Solitude.* It is because Salman Rushdie has employed the same mode of magic realism to describe the past sixty years of Indian history, giving all the details of events of the subcontinent. According to Salman Rushdie, fantasy or magic realism has developed out of surrealism. He also writes that it expresses a genuinely 'Third World Consciousness'. This fantasy is used by the postcolonial migrant writers like Rushdie to recreate history. He has achieved all this in *Midnight's Children.* In this novel, Rushdie has used various modes such as levitation, flights, telepathy, drums, memories, magic potions, inevitability, and transformation of matter into mind to depict the phantasmagorical realities of post-Independent India.

This postcolonial India also has hallucination, insanity, extraordinary situations as the norms of life. *Midnight's Children* confirms the elements of magical and the real, the mimetic and the marvellous. The chief protagonist of the novel or his narrator describes things both real and unreal. The beginning of the novel starts with a narration that seems real because of authentication with the help of 'time', 'dates', and 'place', which is to establish the nation's history. It also seems as though there are chunks of historical facts from the texts for the readers. Similarly, there is much more of the narration that establishes the fact that it is a fantasy. In the novel, there is a purposeful intermingling of the recognisably realistic with the unexpected and the inexplicable, the elements of dream or fairy tale mingle with the everyday life events, and also keep a balanced tone to project the objective realistic reports; at the same time, making space for the fantastic. Saleem states that he has become the apex of an isosceles triangle, supported by the wild god of memory (Fantasy), and the wild god of the present (Realistic) (150). It is at the end of the novel that the narrator says 'that one day the world may taste the pickles of history'. According to critics, looking at India through the fragmented mirrors, a multiple image develops. The three generations of the Sinai family are intertwined with the nation's history. Saleem narrates the multitudinous life of Padma, his mistress. Padma is described as the mistress of time (*Midnight's Children*, p. 195). In this novel along with fantasy, time also plays an important role – time and the chief protagonist are in a typical dialogical interrogating relationship.

Saleem Sinai is portrayed as an eccentric narrator. While he narrates the various incidents related to other characters, he makes it a point to slip into those characters in a 'metonymical' action of replacement. The thousand and one children born on 15 August 1947 are no single individuals but fragmented mirror images of the narrator. It is he who had the ability to look into the hearts and mind of other people. Here fantasy makes the unreal seem real. Fantasy is another form – invisibility or vanishing, it seems to be a characteristic feature throughout the novel. There are many incidents of disappearance narrated in the novel, Saleem himself having declared, 'I in a basket, disappeared'. Saleem is said to have the power of a genie, so do the other children born on the same night. They are said to have the power of transmutation, flight, prophecy and wizardry ... (*Midnight's Children,* p. 200).

It is with the help of fantasy that Rushdie is able to split his characters into doubles and multiples. Saleem is both the first, second and third person. Shiva is the alter ego of Saleem, as is Parvati of Jamila. Apart from fantasy, time also plays a pivotal role in the novel. The split is so visible in the fragmented narration that linear time sequence is exploded and time past and time future are both suspended into an eternal 'time present'.

The 'hole' recurs throughout the novel. It is a very important thing, Saleem's mother too was affected, and it was because she could not love her husband in full, as she had learnt to love him in parts, in segments, separately. Saleem even feels the hole at the centre of himself (*Midnight's Children,* p. 193). Even people gather to see Saleem's sister Jamila singer through the hole on the street (*Midnight's Children,* p. 313). Saleem even dreams of his grand-father looking down at him through the hole in a perforated cloud (*Midnight's Children,* p. 46). Saleem tours the whole of India through the peephole of a private 'Dilli Dekho' machine. There after, he declares that the history of the nation is intertwined with his personal life. The hole becomes codified to a symbol which is surreal and supernatural at the same time. It is with the help of this supernatural hole that Rushdie opens up the gap between the signifier and the signified, and between the relations of signs to that meaning is hollowed out and Rushdie's fiction becomes one of semantic excess and semantic vanity.

For Rushdie, the 'real' is not the absolute signified; the humanities of 'reality' are built on prejudices, misconceptions and ignorance as well as on perceptiveness and knowledge *(Imaginary Homelands*, p. 25).

According to critics, Rushdie wishes to emphasis the indeterminacy of reality as the spectral region in this novel and it is located at the praxis. Reality always depends upon the individual perception of things. As one moves from the past to the present, the concrete and the plausible become more incredible. According to Rushdie, no individual can perceive the whole truth as 'we are not gods, but wounded creatures, cracked bones, capable only of fractured perceptions' (*Imaginary Homelands,* p. 12), and also that this is the result of a cultural displacement.

IX

Reality that one finds in the novel *Midnight's Children* can always have metaphysical content that does not make it real. The thousand and one children born brought with them 1,001 possibilities which had never been present in one place at one time before, and also there were 1,001 dead-ends. Rushdie has used fantasy as a device, to highlight or project the dynamics of the realistic. Rushdie has liberated his protagonist from the shackles of time. Gradually, he absorbs the clock time, ebbs away and flows with the incidents narrated. However, it can be ascertained that Rushdie's *Midnight's Children* is a postmodern fantasy. Rushdie in his writings has written fabulous historiography of India, especially *Midnight's Children,* and it has been done with a special blend of fantasy. This fantasy has the chutnification of history. Rushdie has followed the masters of fantasy – and fabulist writings like that of Stern Gogoli, Gunter Grass, Gabriel Garcia Marquez, and James Joyce, to name a few. *Midnight's Children* reveals that 'marginality of the migrant' is coined with a double inscription, cross-pollination and hybridisation. In this novel, Rushdie has beautifully super-imposed the past over the present and in clear terms highlighted the fantastic to be a mode of expressing the realist. These two are the most important variations of his idea to work upon this land of mysteries, which has also been termed by Winston Churchill 'a mere geographical expression'. In reality, Churchill meant to say that there is no other country in the world which shall embrace the extraordinary mixture of ethnic groups, the diversity of religions and cultural practices, and the range of levels of economic development that India does (Tharoor, 1997). In this novel, Rushdie has tried to do the same thing by highlighting his idea, it is the true amalgamation of fantasy and reality.

To conclude, Saleem Sinai's life embodies India's dream of independence as well as the devastating effects of a colonial legacy. The text is about India's transition from British colonialism to independence, and from independence to the postcolonial period. The postcolonial struggle for identity is reflected in the character of Saleem Sinai, who is a Hindu child brought up by wealthy Muslims. In the beginning of the novel, he informs us that he is falling apart. In terms of this pitiable psychic physical degeneration, he takes up the task of writing his life story. Incidentally, he writes the story of the degeneration of India as a nation. His dilemma is projected against the backdrop of the early years of independence, the partition of India and Pakistan, and the emergence of 'The Widow' Indira Gandhi, war and the imposition of martial law. This is how Rushdie mixes up the magical thinking with the political reality. This accompanies his unique prose style, which is characterised by acrobatics of rhyme, alliteration, pawn, wordplay and 'Babu' English. The novel is a historical document of modern India. It is a multilayered text that posits Saleem in every significant incident that occurred in the Indian subcontinent during the span of thirty years after independence. This is how Rushdie combines the self-awareness of the narrator with the national identity. He displays how the national events can influence perceptions and our world view. Saleem is born at the stroke of midnight on 15 August 1947 and India became a free nation. It helps us to realise the fact that we are the product of our culture and the surrounding political reality. It allows us to interpret the events in our own way and store them in our memory in order that we define our identity in the light of the ever-changing reality. In this process, we develop our assertions of truth, which are shrouded by certain illusions. Rushdie's mystic reality is a brilliant device to depict the mysticism of the human situation. We are all the products of our conscious and unconscious perceptions, memory, emotional reflections and associations of varied incidents. The external manifestations of changing events collide with the meaning and content of our existence. The text presents a comprehensive, dramatic enactment of Saleem's life. It is a life projected within the changing backdrop of national scenario, of family, friends, loved ones, enemies, passions, psychic fears and cherished dreams. He is constantly changing in his awareness, which constitutes the essence of reality. The complexity of Saleem as a character is understood in the light of the understanding of the complex national identity of postcolonial India. In this process, Rushdie invents and re-creates the history of the nation. He tells the story of the nation through the story of a person. The result is that Rushdie goes beyond history, leading us to the territory of art. This is how the author liberates the truth from the limited area of history.

3 Quest for an Indian Identity

Seth's *A Suitable Boy*

Several modern and postmodern Indian novelists have made attempts to project the idea of a nation and to construct the image of India in their works. For example, Bankim Chandra's idea of a nation in his novel *Anandamath* is nationalistic and idealistic, for which the novel takes the form of a romance. Although it is a novel about a nation, his attitudes to nation are strikingly different from that of Salman Rushdie or Arundhati Roy or Vikram Seth. In case of Rushdie, the idea of the nation has become more problematic. Between Bankim Chandra and Rushdie, there is a fundamental difference in terms of technique, because Rushdie makes use of magic realism or epic realism. Bankim Chandra constructs a romantic image of India as a nation. But Rushdie, Arundhati Roy and Vikram Seth have projected the image of a problematic India in a more problematic way. These problematic areas are linked with Orientalism, Colonialism and Postcolonialism. Orientalism is the construct of the East by the West. The Western rulers constructed a colonial design to exercise their superiority over the East. In fact, the problem of colonialism raises the complex issues that involve the image of India as a nation. For example, Arundhati Roy, in *The God of Small Things*, has been primarily preoccupied with place. She interprets history in terms of place. The novel is an attempt to interpret the history of the Christian community. In this sense, this is a typical Malayalam novel written in English. The issues are deeply rooted in the native soil. She is preoccupied with familial relations between a brother and a sister. But these things do not exist in the West. Similarly, Vikram Seth is much preoccupied with marriage, family and domestic issues. Moreover, he has adopted the vast epic background for his narrative device. The concept of history, place, family and nation are intertwined in the works of these novelists. However, there might be some differences with regard to the individual authors who might attach more importance to any one of the issues. In the opinion of Cielo G. Festino, 'the map of the city of Brahmpur ... has proved a useful literary device to help us visualise how Indian postcolonial novels, such as *A Suitable Boy*, narrate the complex social geography of the postcolonial nation-state' (Prasad, 2005: 169).

II

The question arises how novelists like Rushdie, Roy and Seth resist colonialism while constructing the image of India. The answer to these questions is realised in terms of the evolving language or the discourse. These novelists do not merely use English language as English writers, but they transform the language and give it a distinct form or shape to suit their own purpose. In this sense, the attempt undertaken by these novelists to experiment with language is a form of resistance to British colonialism. Here, we can always talk about the way language has been twisted by these authors in fulfilling their needs. Rushdie very aptly puts it down as 'chutnification of history'. This technique was also used by Arundhati Roy and Vikram Seth in their novels, because they have always wanted to use language as one of the native languages.

It is quite often said by various critics and readers that Seth very ardently followed George Eliot, Thomas Hardy and even Tolstoy. It is also highlighted by many that in *A Suitable Boy,* Seth had to offer a complete blend or concoction of the fiction which is quite typical in itself, having historical characters and events. Now, when we talk of language, Seth has a role model. It is none other than Walter Scott, who is instrumental in setting standards for the nineteenth century historical novels, where we have the location of imagined characters which have real historical events inside along with some real figures. All these finally culminate into one thing, i.e., how individual destinies are shaped by the bigger forces within the society. The society, which stands like a rock, is trying to resist all things that are unacceptable. Critics have put ample light while comparing Seth with Scott in respect of the use of language.

Although we have *A Suitable Boy* written in English, Seth has succeeded in constructing a situation where the readers are forced to imagine that all the different characters speak different languages. In other words, the characters are multilingual. Similarly, in the novels of Walter Scott, a typical situation is constituted where the characters give prominence to multilingual reality, which is expressed through English language. Then there's a comparison between Salman Rushdie's *Midnight's Children* and Vikram Seth's *A Suitable Boy* in their use of English as a translation from other Indian languages, and English as a linguistic choice just to reveal the secularism of their representation of India. The very use of English as a medium to narrate the nation implies a secularising discourse which helps construct and imagine national community, which converges on citizenship and democracy and imaginings of a nation based on religion, caste and language differences. It is observed in these novels that there are many different languages that circulate in the dialogues among characters as they do not speak English as their first language. The use of English by Seth and Rushdie represents the multilingual complexity of the Indian nation, all within the narrative discourse. Mikhail Bakhtin, with his formation of the concept of heteroglossia, shows the interrelation between the different languages, and dialects therein. Salman Rushdie and Vikram Seth went on to reflect their language as the multilingual nature of the Indian nation-state, where unity is not based on a simple national language like in Europe. It is also observed that in Seth's *A Suitable Boy*, there are stylistic elements which crop up from the Indian setting as well as the tradition of Indian literature. There are also traces of the great novels of the eighteenth and nineteenth century Europe. As discussed earlier in this chapter, English is not used by these novelists as English writers but in a different form altogether to suit their own needs.

Salman Rushdie has many times argued that English should not be treated as something that is thrust upon by the colonial forces, but as something by now a naturalized, Indian language. He also writes in an essay of 1983 entitled 'Commonwealth Literature does not Exist', that the children of independent India seem not to think of English as being irredeemably tainted by its colonial provenance. They use it as an Indian language, as one of the tools they have to handle in the right perspective. In India, English is an essential language not only because it makes it possible for two Indians to talk in a language which neither hates. People of India are now making the language as the people of other postcolonial nations. The people who are once colonized by the language are now rapidly making it. They are in turn helped by the language's huge flexibility and size, people are also carving out areas for themselves in its own arena or frontiers. According to Rushdie, English has become an Indian language. Its colonial origin is no more, just like Urdu and unlike all other Indian languages, it has no regional platform, so in a way it has become universal in India. English has acquired in the South an air of lingua-franca, a kind of cultural neutrality.

English in India is now an Indian language and it is viewed as neutralized and non-territorial. Vikram Seth has put up a similar comparison with Sanskrit in his novel *A Suitable Boy*. Again, the reference to Sanskrit is made by one of the characters. Presumably, both Seth and Rushdie's texts promote an objectivist, non-communalist model of language use which denies any emotional and spontaneous differentiation between English and well-established Indian languages. As described by Rushdie, English as an 'Indian language remains problematic, although English in India is the language of most important newspapers and the information and technology sector.' A small negligible section of the populace understands it. There is always doubt in the minds of writers who have tried to express themselves in English regarding the Indianness of the language.

Vikram Chandra falls in line with Ramanujan and also Rushdie and views it as a lingua franca or as one 'Indian language' among other languages spoken in India. India has always been diverse as regards language, culture and religion, multilingualism. Seth's *A Suitable Boy* displays one aspect of Indian diversity. This also highlights Seth's attempt to conserve the diversity of India, where we have an India which is multicultural. It has many religions and is a multilingual society. According to Seth, *A Suitable Boy* is an alibi for religious tolerance, but India is a country where since ages we have the Hindu-Muslim conflict as a burning topic or a topic for discussion. It may be the political alliance of Mahesh Kapoor and the Nawab or the friendship between Maan and Firoz and the difficulties that followed. Even the communal riots that were a blot in Indian politics and that disfigured Brahmpur, or Lata's doomed love for Kabir, the Muslim student in her class, appears as the strands of this burning topic. According to scholars who have worked extensively on Seth and his novel *A Suitable Boy*, it may be described as a novel that has the capability to take in a quadrilingual reality. The characters are represented as speaking, understanding, reading and writing varied combination of four main languages of the time, namely Hindi, Bengali, Urdu and English. There is yet another facet to it, and it is the linguistic and cultural diversity in the Western world. This is evident from the three other languages that feature in the background. Sanskrit and Arabic act as cultural references for Hindu and Muslim communities. German acts as another language for reference, which is the native tongue of Hans, the diplomat fiancé of Kakoli Chatterjee.

It is observed that there is an interaction between the four languages and the fourth has a stigma of the departed colonizers. It is also observed that the communication theme, essential to this novel, also embraces the domain of music, and also elsewhere in Seth's work, music plays a key role as a mode of human interaction running parallel to language.

III

The status of English in India has always been accepted as problematic, much before Independence, and shall continue to be so in the years to come. The use of English as an alien language for native purposes is not new. Since before the coming of the British, even Persian played a similar role during the days of the Mughal rulers in India. Although the very mode of formation of discussion dates back to the period of the Raj, interaction between English and Indian languages is parallel to the interaction between the other regional languages as well. A significant work has been done in this regard by noted Bengali writer and critic Amit Choudhury in his book, which can be called a seminal anthology of 2001 *The Picador Book of Modern Indian Literature*. This anthology may be taken as quite significant as it takes in both English medium material and also translations from many Indian languages. These include many texts of substantial cultural significance, and are witness to the complex nature of subcontinental language issues. This is the same thing that Vikram Seth has done in his novel. He employs four languages simultaneously, namely English, Urdu, Bengali and Hindi, in among his characters. They use the language in the appropriate places and for appropriate purposes. Time and again Rushdie has insisted that English should not be treated as something that has been thrust upon us by the British but as one other, by now naturalised, Indian language.

In the novel, the main interaction is between the four languages, out of which two are purely Indian, one is Arabic and English bears the stigma of the just departed colonisers. All the four languages used in the novel have different roles to play. Hindi appears as a potentially dominant national institutional tongue, Urdu plays the pivotal role of the cultural maker of the Indian post-Partition Muslim community. Bengali is termed the bearer of aesthetics and the arts of precisely Indian modern group, while English is the lingua franca.

Gradually, as the story proceeds, we come across the complexities of these four languages. There may be different facets to it; first we talk of the political facet. The story originates in a North Indian state well within a Hindi-speaking belt, and where people and politicians are struggling hard to make it the sole official language. In such a situation, the position of Urdu and English suddenly becomes problematic. In reality, all the people and the naturalised Hindi speakers were quite comfortable with that language as well. The minister Mahesh Kapoor's dilemma over language is depicted much during the initial pages of the novel:

> 'Mahesh Kapoor himself found it very difficult to read the Purva Pradesh Legislative debates of the last few years … . The real difficulty was that Mahesh Kapoor was not very familiar with the Hindi or Devanagari-script. He had been brought up at a time when boys were taught to read the Urdu or Arabic script. In the 1930s the Proceedings of the Protected Provinces Legislative Assembly were printed speech by speech in English, Urdu and Hindi depending on the language that the speaker wrote or spoke. His own speeches were printed in Urdu … . The English speeches he could read without difficulty. But he tended to skip the Hindi ones, as they made him struggle. Now, after Independence, the Proceedings were printed entirely in the official language of the State, which was Hindi. Urdu speeches too were printed in Hindi script and English could only be spoken and that too, with the permission of the Speaker of the House. That was why Mahesh Kapoor often asked his wife to read out the debates to him. She had been taught like many women of the time, to read and write under the influence of the Hindu revivalist organisation, the Arya Samaj. The script that she had been taught was, the script of the ancient Sanskrit texts and the modern Hindi language'.

The minister Mahesh Kapoor had no idea of the importance of the language that people are to get it changed to official language. It was also discovered that his wife did not know English. Even his Sub-Divisional Officer Sandeep Lahiri did not like the very language Hindi, and was not very fluent in it. The language problem also surfaced in the Assembly when there was a debate on the pro- Hindi Language Bill in the Purva Pradesh Legislative Assembly; a number of ideological-linguistic positions expressed, which began from culturalists to the anti-colonial to the apparently pragmatic. There is a character in the novel Begum Abida Khan, a defender of the

Muslim cause and the community at large who protests discrimination saying 'the sudden enforcement of Hindi in the Devanagari script has closed the doors of government service on the Muslims', and asks: 'If a foreign language like English can be tolerated …, why can Urdu not be tolerated?' She concludes that Urdu 'can be treated like any other regional language. But it must not be dispossessed'. Urdu had a very precarious position in Purva Pradesh, but still the plot of the novel is such that it makes it the cultural badge of the Muslim community through ghazals composed by great Urdu poets and sung by the courtesan Saeeda Bai. The language has had such an impact that a person like Maan Kapoor, having a relationship with Saeeda Bai, is forced to learn Urdu so that he can communicate well. Subsequently, Maan gets an Urdu instructor, struggles a lot with the alphabets. Now, whatever maybe the fate of different languages in India and how so important they may become, it can be deduced from *A Suitable Boy's* fictional world that English shall not disappear from India. Howsoever much patronage Hindi gets from political spheres and the strong cultural pull of Urdu and Bengali, English shall continue to be the lingua franca for easy communication between different groups. The realities described are of quadrilingual nature; Seth has forced more challenges than Walter Scott. Gradually, English has crept into the novel through its characters. Further it is noteworthy that the command that Vikram Seth displays over English language is with regard to multiple registers. According to late R.K. Narayan, in one of his interviews to *India Today*: 'Vikram Seth shows absolute mastery of the English language'. This was meant for The Golden Gate, but is equally applicable to *A Suitable Boy*. Now, when we make an analysis of the use of English by Seth in three different works, we find *The Golden Gate* is written in American English, *An Equal Music* in British English and *A Suitable Boy* in Indian English.

IV

It was seen that within a decade from 1980–1990, there were many Indian English works of fiction making their way to the British and American book markets. The writers who made their mark on the scene were Salman Rushdie with his *Midnight's Children*, Arundhati Roy with *The God of Small Things* and Seth's *A Suitable Boy* have been viewed as a cultural translation and the effect it has on the readers rather than the writing technique. According to Maria Tymoczko these kinds of translations provide an analogy to postcolonial writings (Prasad, 2005; Srivastava, 2005). In this sense cultural translation can be treated as a metaphor for 'the postcolonial.' The postcolonial experience of the people of the Third World countries provide more interest as a recurring subject for the readers of the First World countries rather than techniques employed in there novels.

When we take into account the linguistic aspect, this novel presents a wide panorama of Indian society in the years soon after Independence. This colonial novel narrates the intertwining lives and relationship, spanning eighteen months. The narrative covers a cross-section of people, families who are connected to Brahmpur, the imaginary North Indian city. The narrative is guided by a very traditional theme of searching for a husband for 'Lata', who is a student of English literature. Lata now considers the claims of three rival contenders before she could make her final choice. The novel by Vikram Seth not only tries to explore the Indian society after the Raj, in all its multiple political, religious, cultural and communal ramifications, but also raises a wide range of issues relating to various aspects of language and communication. According to M. Rajgopalachary and B. Krishna Chandra Keerthi, in their writing *Social Comedy in the Nineteenth Century British Tradition*, by evoking Jane Austen, Vikram Seth is constricting to the magic realist form pioneered by Salman Rushdie and gradually refined by authors like Vikram Chandra and Amitav Ghosh.

In this novel, one important feature is multilingualism, which appears as one of the aspects of the diversity of India. The author has a moral duty and commitment to preserve that diversity throughout – Indian multicultural society is multi-religious and a multilingual society. Seth argues that 'it is insult to Hinduism that these people have hijacked what it means to be Hindu. It is tolerance, understanding – not just trying to bash your neighbour over the head because he is Muslim. These things need to be said'.

There is a constant recurrence of Hindu-Muslim tension all through the novel. This comes to surface in different forms whether it is the break-up of the political alliance broken between Mahesh Kapoor and Nawab Sahib, or the difficulties arising out of the friendship between Maan and Firoz, or the communal riots of Brahmpur and finally, Lata's doomed passion for Kabir.

Multilingualism in this novel appears as one of the important aspects of the diversity of India. 'In this context of a strained plurality of Seth's representation *A Suitable Boy* may be described as a novel that takes in a quadrilingual reality'. The novel presents a wide panorama of the Indian society, soon after Independence. The colossal novel narrates the intertwining lives and relationships, over a period of eighteen months. According to Italian scholar Silvia Albertazzi, 2000 ('Vikram Seth has been called by some critics, a little exaggeratedly, the new Tolstoy, thanks to the range and scope of his narrative ... a panorama of situations and characters, frequently interconnected which provide the fullest possible picture of India in the wake of independence – the triumph of the nation as "imagined community"). Seth has been able to bring forth the real image of India. According to another prominent critic of Europe Georg Lukács, 'great realism and popular humanism are merged into an organic unity'. Lukács writes that great realist novelists 'penetrate deeply into the great universal problems of their time and inexorably depict the true essence of reality as they see it'; and such claims may convincingly be made for Vikram Seth's vast, all-encompassing fictional model of a great nation at a crucial moment of historical development (Rollason, p. 64).

As regards language, the characters speak, understand and write four main languages, namely Hindi, Bengali, Urdu and English. There are a few other languages as well which can be called reference languages, like Sanskrit and Arabic, German being the native tongue of Hans, the diplomat and Kakoli Chatterjee's fiancé. This highlights the linguistic and cultural diversity of the world that has been projected by Vikram Seth in his novel *A Suitable Boy*.

It is seen that in two of his novels, namely *Waverly* (1814) and *Rob Roy* (1818), Walter Scott has experimented with the plot of a triangular society. The pattern of writing quite appropriately suits Vikram Seth. The two novels highlighted the period when Scotland was ruled by the British. The society depicted here had on its own split into the modern, developed the Lowlands and Highlands where the clans still thrive.

There is a difference which is presumably most striking in itself between Rushdian form of writing and Seth's. Vikram Seth has adopted the classical realist form of writing his fiction, whereas Rushdie banks upon magic realism. The methodology put in by Vikram Seth is diametrically opposite to the one followed by Rushdie, that of magic realism. The fiction of Seth is all based on classical realism. *A Suitable Boy* is reminiscent of Victorian realism. His novel paints his protagonists' private concerns on a public canvas. The assumption that Seth was deeply influenced by George Eliot is perceived within the text itself when we find one of the characters Amit Chatterjee at one point of time declaring, 'I still bear the scars of Middlemarch' (*A Suitable Boy,* p. 1254). This is a clear indication of the influence that George Eliot has on Seth. This reference is to Eliot's 1872 novel by the same name. *Middlemarch* is just like Seth's Brahmpur, completely fictitious in nature. Seth has also put in place Thomas Hardy, when one of the characters Haresh reads Hardy, and also has volumes of Hardy's novels neatly displayed in the living room. Hardy is yet another shining star whom Seth follows as regards giving local names in his works. The reference strengthens the fact in Seth's narrative in the English tradition of the nineteenth century. The position that English language commands in India has been taken as problematic, and it is well beyond independence.

It is also found that Seth not only follows Hardy in giving local names to places (fictitious), but also shares ground with the great South Indian novelist R.K. Narayan, who provides a panoramic view of small towns in South India. There is similarity between Narayan's Malgudi and those names given to towns, and cities by Seth, but Narayan has expertise in myths whereas Seth does not. According to Pico Iyer, R.K. Narayan, Vikram Seth and Rohinton Mistry can be put into one strand of Indian English literature – 'Compassionate Realism'. As far as Seth and Rushdie are concerned, Seth is realistic but unlike Rushdie he does not use 'magic realism' as part of his realistic move in explaining things. Rushdie puts more stress on jugglery of language, whereas Seth is far from it.

Tolstoy had made Napoleon immortal in his novel *War and Peace*. Similarly, in *A Suitable Boy*, Vikram Seth also has put in a combination of a hybrid blend of a fiction but typical historical characters and events. He has put in real efforts to invent the main characters, but has also put historical events. The fictional characters like the politician Mahesh Kapoor and the CM, S.S. Sharma, are reading out a real letter sent by Jawaharlal Nehru to all the chief ministers on 9 August 1951. We have, though for a brief period, J.L. Nehru appearing in the scene and thereby affecting the electoral campaign. The locals named by Seth have some connection with history somewhere. The city of Brahmpur and the state of Purva Pradesh do not exist in reality. Italian writer Italo Calvano in his book *Invisible Cities* writes about such ghost cities, but here we shall not talk about such cities. The cities and states mentioned by Seth are not vague ones. Rather, Purva Pradesh is found in North India and well within the Hindu belt. Similarly, Brahmpur is found on the banks of the Ganges. The state, though imaginary, has a convincing historical background, and is also linked to the other real states and provinces in India that were under the British rule. Brahmpur was spelt by the British as Brahmpore, and the state of Purva Pradesh was Protected Provinces. Quite similar to the scenario in India, the state has post-Partition a considerable chunk of Muslim and Urdu-speaking people.

In *A Suitable Boy*, there is a mix of facts with fiction, and it is a complex exercise on the part of the author. The fictional city of Brahmpur is a hybrid creation of many North Indian cities like Varanasi, Agra and even Ayodhya. The city of Varanasi refers to the festival on the Ganges; Agra has its reference to the leather industry, which is mentioned in the novel. Ayodhya is connected to the Babri Masjid controversy of 1910.

Contemporary South Asian literature has always tried to struggle with the rising religious intolerance and fundamental politics in the Indian subcontinent. Example can be given of Salman Rushdie's *The Moor's Last Sigh*, Amitav Ghosh's *The Shadow Lines*, and Shashi Tharoor's *Riots*. The books mentioned suggest the widespread South Asian concern with the present-day communal conflicts. There are books which express a deep concern for the growing fanaticism in India, especially in the Eighties and Nineties. All these have had a dramatic effect and brought to the forefront the crisis confronting the secular postcolonial Indian state. In the book *A Suitable Boy*, Seth has tried in a different way to highlight the treatment of the interreligious romance that loosely lies at the centre of the novel. The stage is set in the imaginary town of Brahmpur in the fictional province of Purva Pradesh, which can be easily identified with a Hindi-speaking province. During the days of the British, it was termed the Protected Provinces. And the time is from 1950 and 1952.

The novel relates the doomed Hindu-Muslim relationship or the romance of Lata and Kabir. It was against the backdrop of communal tensions, land reforms and the first general elections after Independence. The relationship that was just at the initiation stage between Lata and Kabir comes to an abrupt end just when the identity of Kabir becomes known. The first thing that comes in between is the social taboo against Hindu-Muslim marriage. But, love transcends over all matters of differences of culture, class, reforms, race or caste. Still, it is not acceptable to the upper class Hindu family. Such a relationship is not only unacceptable, it is unspeakable and unthinkable.

Seth projects Rupa Mehra, the mother of Lata, as one of the representatives of her class, caste and generation. Lata is taken to Calcutta by her mother, and then begins the quest for a Suitable Boy. The quest for a suitable boy scans through entire northern India and also eastern India. The story revolves around the upper caste affluent urban population. Subsequently, Lata meets Amit, a Bengali-English speaking poet – (he has a colonial hangover) – and Haresh. A shoe executive is Mrs Mehras choice for Lata. Finally, Lata decides to abandon Amit and marry Haresh, keeping with her mother's desires. Lata disavows Kabir not because of anything else but because of her family's opposition to Hindu-Muslim relationship. The final conclusion of the romance was not termed a failure. In this novel, cross-cultural desire has been deployed as a way of bringing cultural, religious or racial boundaries within the nation as well as across national borders.

Peter Hulme, in his writing, demonstrates how such love plots articulate as the ideals of cultural hegemony through romance. When we consider the tradition of Indian writing in English, *The God of Small Things* by Arundhati Roy is the famous example of this literary convention in this novel. Romance figures between the upper caste Syrian Christian women and the untouchable Paravan, Velutha. There are many examples of intercommunity desire – even in Salman Rushdie's *The Moor's Last Sigh*. We have intercommunity desire, where Rushdie celebrates 'cultural hybridity', and 'intermixing' as a way of transgressing the boundaries of different communities. There are even certain films against the backdrop of literary and cinematic conventions that must be examined so as to link them to Seth's representation of the Lata-Kabir relationship.

The cultural hegemony that Peter Hulme talks about is nothing but 'a concept coined by Marxist philosopher Antonio Gramsci. This means that a diverse culture can be ruled or dominated by one group or class, that everybody practices and shared beliefs provide the foundation for complex systems of domination'. Gramsci in his theory of hegemony argued after a proper and through analysis that 'the failure of the workers to make an anti-capitalist revolution was due to the successful capture of the workers' ideology, self-understanding, and organisation by hegemonic culture'. The analysis of hegemony or 'rule' was also formulated by Antonio Gramsci. Hegemony was portrayed as a complex layering of the social structures. It can also be discussed that the perspective of the ruling class has been absorbed by the populace or the masses of workers. In the economically advanced industrial societies, hegemonic cultural innovations like compulsory schooling, mass media, and popular culture had indoctrinated workers to a false consciousness. Thereby, these workers paid much attention to the high sounding rhetoric of the leaders and were seeking consumer opportunities to get idle class status. They also tried to embrace an individualistic ethos of success through competition, and or accepting the guidance of bourgeois religious leaders. According to Gramsci, hegemony, which is a complex layering of social structures of society, has individual 'mission' and internal logic. This again allows its members to behave in a particular way, which is different from the other. Wherever there is layered hegemony, the individual common sense, which is fragmented, is quite effective in helping people deal with small everyday activities.

The story of Seth represents something that is taking place between a Muslim man and a Hindu woman. It signifies the interreligious romance of Bombay films, which more often tends to figure the heterosexual relationship between the representative male Hindu secular nationalist self and the exotic gendered burkha-clad Muslim subject. The romance of Lata and Kabir is set in post-Partition or post-Independence Brahmpur. The novel attempts to represent India as a great crowd, a throng, tainted with *India: A Million Mutinies Now* (1990) where Naipaul has correctly intuited and made his theme, the rise of long-supposed identities that radically altered the Indian society in this decade.

Lata and Kabir represent the two nations of India and Pakistan as two separate entities. Their ill-fated romance is set against a backdrop of communal conflict in the post-Partition era. India has been represented as discussed earlier as a crowd, a throng having an epic scale, where several acts of group violence are seen. In the novel, Seth has in his own way treated the two moments, of religious violence and religious conflicts, which is common in India. This has given rise to the two Hindu riots of the Eighties and the Nineties in India. The two riots have been placed by Seth miles apart but still they can be seen framing the Lata-Kabir romance, even though they do not directly impinge upon the trajectory of the romance. These two riots are set against the backdrop of Hindu revivalist movement headed by two most important national leaders of India. People like Raja of Maoh and L.N. Agarwal, the Congress Home Minister of Purva Pradesh. Seth has always tried and kept alive a kind of religious conflict. He has purposefully constructed a scenario where there is a dispute between a historic mosque that stands on the site of a Shiva temple. This is a fictional reconstruction of the Babri Masjid carnage. A Hindu Raja represents a Hindu nationalist movement of the early Fifties. The Raja also has links with the Muslim courtesans like Saeeda Bai, and plans to build a Shiva temple. It will be built on the ruins of the earlier Shiva temple where Aurangzeb has built a mosque.

In the novel, there is an omniscient narrator, just like Saleem Sinai of *Midnight's Children*. Finally, the foundation stone-laying ceremony leads to the clash of ideas and paves the way for the riots. Seth has also demonstrated how the fundamentalist discourse plays a role in the transformation and crystallization of religious identities in and above all identities in moments of conflicts.

Apart from religious conflicts, we also have caste conflicts in the same locale of Brahmpur, between the traders of Misri Mandi and the shoemakers who are Jats by caste. Policemen are deployed in large numbers to curb the uprising. There is the colonial stance of hegemony, and social hegemony engaged in the domination of low-caste people. A small group of security personnel guards the mosque and the temple in case riots break out. It so happens that the police are forced to open fire at the minority Muslims and the state administration is blamed for sheer mismanagement of the situation. The narrator here declares that some riots are caused, some bring themselves into being (*A Suitable Boy,* p. 245). It indicates that the Hindu nationalists and the State are the inevitable features for the communal uprising of religious intolerance. The first riot was due to the failure of the State to check those elements who abated the uprising, but the second riot was more 'spontaneous', between the Muharram mourners and the Ramlila celebrators. In his essay, Seth has tried to project the real India where there are some man-made riots and some are not created by man.

According to H.S. Mahapatra and J.N. Nayak, Arundhati Roy has taken cue from James Joyce, Gabriel Garcia Marquez but Salman Rushdie, the exponent of postmodernism of the Indian context, has gone back a few centuries to Laurence Stern. But authors like Vikram Seth, Amitav Ghosh and Vikram Chandra have clung to the English of the nineteenth century. *A Suitable Boy* is also termed a 'European novel' by Seth's agent Giles Gordon. It is anachronistic in a sense that it has recalled a phase of European realism. In a sense, history has been made real or the past has been dealt as present. In *A Suitable Boy,* Seth has recast the nineteenth century English novelistic conventions of Jane Austen, Charles Dickens and George Eliot. Jane Austen has been one of his favourite authors. He has been greatly influenced by this author, as he clarifies this in many discussions and interviews. His 'clear-window' narrative aspirations and his preference for an easy-going, transparent style is derived from Jane Austen. The novel is stuffed with Austenian moments and illusions. This can be analysed when we read the fourth section of the essay. There is ample example of Austenian vocabulary in the text, and they are used at key places of sexual surrender. Darcy in *Pride and Prejudice* (1813) had inspired a kind of gentle sensation in Elizabeth, Lata evokes in Haresh 'tender feelings of the original' (Seth, 1993: 1290). This is the moment in both Austen and Seth that the love cycle is made complete by sealing it off.

It is quite surprising to note that two authors, separated by huge differences of history and culture, could come close to each other. Jane Austen wrote about English landed gentry of the early nineteenth century. Seth also wrote about the middle class, the Indian middle class which unlike the Europeans is a slow riser. This class represented by Seth occupies the centrestage in post-Independent India of the 1950s. The novel of Seth covers the entire India, with an equally matching number of characters. To be precise, the novel is the story of four families: the Kapoors, the Mehras, Chaterjees and the Khans. Haresh Trivedi states that Vikram Seth is a 'later-day Jane Austen' (Trivedi and Mukherjee, 1996: 11). Seth has written a realist novel pitched against the face of pervasive postmodernist doubts about realism. Postmodernism in a way rejects that novels have any access to reality. Postmodernists oppose the mapping function of realism. According to postmodernists, the factors that influence realism, like names places, dates and deictics, create a kind of illusion of reality or a 'reality effect'.

The most striking feature of contemporary Indian English fiction is postmodernism 'magical realism', which strikes a key note in Salman Rushdie's fictions and which he made so immensely popular. Vikram Seth in his novel has tried to create realism about people and places and this is a kind of revolution. This attaches itself to the 'tradition of compassionate realism' which was quite highlighted by Mulk Raj Anand, Raja Rao and R.K. Narayan, keeping away from the 'pin wheeling' experiment of Rushdie. Seth has a particular attachment to the realism of Jane Austen. The whole focus is on the drawing room and the parlour as the possible plan of complex social negotiations and exchange. 'Marriage' happens to be a centre point of discussion both for Seth as well as Austen. The key fact remains, who will be the 'suitable boy' from amongst the host of contenders for the 'girl' (Lata). She is supposed to highlight the values and aspirations of the emergent class, and by doing so steer the nation to a rightful destiny.

Both in the context of Austen and Seth, marriage has a large, social and ideological implication. This key focus on marriage is a part of the process inaugurated by 'domestic fiction'. This is what Nancy Armstrong has argued in her study *Desire and Domestic Fictions* (1987). In her view, this has contributed to feminization of bourgeois culture. According to Nancy Armstrong, 'domestic fiction always centres round domestic women who value marriage and family activity sought to untangle the language of sexual relation from the language of politics, and doing so introduces a new form of political power' (1987: 3). This power can be found in the image of a dehistoricized bourgeois subjectivity. This new form of subjectivity also helped to reinforce patriarchal power relations, and in line with Austen's novel, this difficulty of marriage choice is made clear in terms of the pressure exerted by the patriarchal subjectivity. In the novel of Jane Austen, the heroine dashes out of all kinds of strangleholds and plunges headlong into the vortex of bourgeois patriarchal relations. In *A Suitable Boy*, Lata is justifying her choice of Haresh and it moves along the same lines. She presents it in a bit different way; 'Haresh is practical, he's forceful, he is not cynical, he gets things done and he helps people without making a fuss of it' (Seth, 1993: 1297). *A Suitable Boy* is Austenian in one respect and un-Austenian in another because it is an Indian story. This duality is always there from the very beginning of Indian English novels, this form of writing developed in the nineteenth century and it began by an imitation of the English realist novels which were shadowed by the established and influential form and authority of the colonial ethos. The move towards narration was quite slow and hesitant; they started from reportage and description to narration of a 'plain and unvarnished' kind (Dey, 1874).

The realist tradition in writing still continues to rule the Indian fiction. According to Meenakshi Mukherjee, 'the realist tradition of novel writing subsequently went on to form the mainstream, along which the Indian English novel developed in the twentieth century' (Mukherjee, 1985: 16). Therefore, a contemporary Austenian novel in India is not unusual or preposterous, but the point is that the 'pre-novel' convention of orality, fantasy and circularity continue to animate and inform the modern Indian novel in English (Mohapatra and Nayak, 2005: 29). This can be well traced in the narrative unfolding of *A Suitable Boy*. It is not only based or conceived like an Austenian story of marriage, it also focuses on love, or a rational love which is the only allowable basis of marriage.

The story of Mrs Rupa Mehra's search for a suitable boy for her youngest daughter Lata constitutes the main thematic aspect of the novel. Lata makes love with Kabir, moves about with Amit and finally ends up marrying Haresh Khanna as 'a suitable boy', who was her mother's first choice. The whole process involves Lata's maturation and growth. Although one finds the novel full of married couples finding other lovers, the novel is not only about marriage alone. It is in fact a portrait of India, a few years after Independence, Partition, Jawaharlal Nehru as the Prime Minister, General Elections round the corner, the Congress party trying to find a place for the second term. Campaigning revolves around the abolition of Zamindari system or feudalism. There is a strong political motive behind all this. The story originates from a small provincial settlement of Brahmpur, which is the fictional name of Patna. All the characters are of high profile, the Mehras and

Kapoors are related by matrimony. Savita, eldest daughter of Mrs Rupa Mehra, is married to Pran, eldest son of Mahesh Kapoor. A strong political bond emerges and gives rise to an opposition to the Khans. The Kapoors are the initiators of the Zamindari Abolition Bill, and if made into a law, shall reduce landholding of the largest landowners of the area. Here, we have a huge canvas for the immense horizontal spread of narrative; the multiple stories of individual characters create a sense of complexity and diversity. Lata meets Kabir in the same university where she studies and falls in love. Mann, the youngest son of Mahesh Kapoor, falls in love with Saeeda Bai, a courtesan of Brahmpur. Rasheed is courting Saeeda Bai's daughter Tasneem. All these stories generate more stories and further they help in reinforcing the two plots of Lata and Mann. Along with the changing of lifestyles of the characters, the India they live in also changes, as it enters a modern era. According to Pico Iyer, 'It is the story of the passing of an era, of the last strains of a rarefied world of ghazals and Nawab, and the first approaches of a new, industrial era, of how the elegant Rajput miniature, you may say, is being replaced by the news photo' (Iyer, 1993: 20). The story derives added significance from the fact that it is the same time when we find the story of the freedom and empowerment of a colonial people. This is the time when a huge country undergoes a sea change and unprecedented birth pangs. It is observed by critics that there are plenty of other Austenian qualities that can be attributed to this novel. For example, the novel is not set at a time when there was complete disturbance during Independence; rather, it is set in a period of interval after Independence. The parallel can be drawn in the Austenian stress on personal relationship during the famed Napoleonic wars. The sole purpose in both these contexts is to shift attention from macro history to micro history, and shift the locus of meaning from structure to texture. It is something important to note that family is central to the Indian English novel, both in its regional language and English language as well. According to Vinay Kirpal, 'The family which has been central to Indian English novels ... is aggressively fore-grounded in Indian English postmodern novel. Work after work, it appears almost like a character in *Midnight's Children, The Shadow Lines, The Great Indian Novel, Rich Like Us, A Suitable Boy, Such a Long Journey, The Binding Vine*, and a host of other novels. By contrast, the characters in Euro-American, postmodern novels such as *Catch-22, Possession*, and *Under the Net*, appear to be so alone. No mothers, fathers, sisters, brothers, wives, husbands, sons, daughters, cousins, aunts and uncles; only lovers keep coming in and out of their lives. They inhabit, a lonely society and the malaise of a nation spills into the novels (Mohapatra, 1996: 19).

As a general trend, the families depicted in the Indian English novels are usually Indian middle class families. The family ties or bonds are extremely strong. In *A Suitable Boy*, the family bond and the family tree is so drawn that it almost becomes a preface to the novel. It also becomes the very metaphor for the novel genre itself. Amit, Seth's alter ego in the novel, puts it, 'Sprouts and grows, and trunks or intertwines with other branches' (Seth, 1993: 483). This novel is Austenian in structure and form, having an Indian substance.

As far as realist writing is concerned, Seth and Austen are at par with each other. The realist project of Austen is perceived in terms of technical matter and transparency of language and style. Michael McKeon has a very assertive account of the rise of the novel. According to McKeon, the novel arose in England in the early modern period. The sole purpose of the novel was to deal with two kinds of crisis: epistemological and social. McKeon states that the 'novel addressed itself to the twofold question of how to signify 'truth' and 'virtue' at a time of major social and cultural transition in people's attitude towards these things' (McKeon, 1987).

Critics have found that the novels of Jane Austen completely mould themselves to McKeon's model. Further, in the novels of Austen, we find a juxtaposition of realism and romance, of empiricism and idealism which can be seen to enact a complex ideological differentiation between England and its others. As regards Seth and his *A Suitable Boy*, what critics have found is that Seth is taking much more than Austenian realism with regard to technical aspects of language and style. For him, realism is a means of countering the evasive mode of postmodernist writing.

'Seth is ultimately interested in writing what has been called, a 'counter Rushdie epic' (Iyer, 1993: 20). It is also observed that what Gothicism was for Austen, 'marvellous realism' is for Seth, the effects of realism or the power of realist novel. As far as the Indian realist novels are concerned, 'realist novel is a necessity, not simply because of a panoramic quality or heterogeneity, but also because its very nature directs both writers and readers to history. History that heals as well as hurts or we can say that history which acts as a shaping force'. Seth in his novel has tried to revive realism, since realism is the essential precondition for deploying the novel in its nation-forming role or function. It is clearly seen in the projection of Austenian realism as a ground for narrating the nation in *A Suitable Boy*. Seth has tried to figure out an India which is attached to many things, attached to men, women and history. The history that India is attached to is of the very grassroot level history of everyday events, of eating, drinking, growing up, marrying and finally, dying. According to Edward W. Said, Austen's novels are political, for they all necessarily imply 'questions of power, of justice, questions of wealth, and poverty and so on' (Said, 1996: 11).

According to Pico Iyer, Vikram Seth has been able to achieve the Austenian goal to 'usher India into the drawing room, to make it seem as everyday and close to us as St Petersberg, or, say Regency Bath' (Iyer, 1993: 20). The influence of Austen in the construction of *A Suitable Boy* is evident from the fact that Lata reads 'Emma' in the train during her journey from Calcutta to Kanpur (pp. 586–87). Again, Amit jokingly likens himself to Jane Austen (p. 407), also there is a reference to Mansfield Park towards the end of the novel (p. 1287). Apart from this, there are also references to other writers as well, writers like Thomas Maan, Tennyson, Thomas Hardy, George Eliot and Marel Proust and also William Shakespeare.

The beginning of the novel finds Mrs Rupa Mehra initiating a search for a suitable boy for Lata, by doing this she sets the narration rolling and works out the logic of the Austenian: 'It is a truth universally acknowledged ...'. Mrs Rupa Mehra is inclined towards Haresh, whom she likes the most. But, Lata has a different viewpoint. She is young and impulsive and has just formed a relationship with a Muslim boy from the same university, named Kabir. This relationship can be compared to the situation in Jane Austen's *Sense and Sensibility* (1811), where we have a sudden attraction of Marianne towards Willoughby and the disturbance it creates at the end. Here we find that gradually Lata has come to terms with her mother and there is a change of attitude on Lata's part. The novel drifts slowly from Lata being the impetuous kind towards the kind of attraction to a 'calmer, less frantic love' (Seth, 1993: 1299). In this novel, we find a constant tension between realism and romance, as in the case of Austen.

There is ample evidence of Jane Austen's influence on Seth and his work. There is a kind of parallel situation going between Austen and Seth. The most important aspect of Austen's novel is to generate 'consent'. *A Suitable Boy* is about the emergent middle class of the newly independent nation, and that the nation undertakes to celebrate the middle class ethos, then the importance on consent is quite inevitable. Although we have three contenders for Lata, one with whom she falls in love (Kabir), the other with whom Lata flirts (Amit), and the third whom Lata finally marries is Haresh. Here we see that Haresh represents the perfect blend of reason and emotion. In the process of highlighting Haresh, Seth has gone far ahead by even saying at one place, 'No poet worked harder or more inspired to craft a poem than Haresh worked for the next three days on his pair of shoes' (Seth, 1993: 920). Here, Seth is trying to bring out the parallel between the poet and the artisan. He is actually trying to bring out the realistic aspects of the pre-industrial era's unity of work and art. This highlights Seth's conceptualization of the realistic aesthetics, which is central for him throughout. As regards parallelism of writing mode, Seth's *A Suitable Boy* and Austen's *Persuasion* (1818) both open with the same style with an ironic portrayal of 'the vanity of person and of situation' (Austen, 1983: 1145). Mrs Rupa Mehra is afloat by glorifying her late husband's status in the government service, and his age-old days in the Indian Railways. Similarly, Sir Walter highlights his obsession with his 'baronetage'. The most important thing that comes out of both Austen and Seth's novel' is that Lata and Anne Elliot move against the patriarchal order with their own marriage choices. But, something comes in between Lata and Haresh, and that is class. Haresh is a middle class, self-made man, and he lacks the so-called refinement and social grace of the covenanted Anglophile elite of new India. Arun, Lata's brother, disapproves of Haresh primarily because of these reasons. First, his English is not good; second, he moves about in inferior social circles, and third, that he does not have a decent government job. The arrangements that were put forth by Arun go back to the days of colonial India, or the days of ascendency of the self-same class. Another similarity in both Austen and Seth is that both Lata and Anne have gone against their persuaders. Lata has gone against Arun and Anne has gone against Lady Russell. Lata decided on the same instance soon after receiving the letter of disapproval from Arun: 'She wrote to Haresh the same evening accepting with gratitude – and indeed, warmth his often repeated offer of marriage' (Seth, 1993: 1295).

It is interesting to note that Lata has selected the path taken by the Austenian heroine in moderating her passion and the path takes her to Haresh. Kabir is branded as a dark force, going against Austenian theory, and this force disrupts logic and reason and makes Lata experience the heart of darkness. There is a nice place of shadow and light while Lata is unconscious of all these happenings (Prasad, 2005; Mohapatra and Nayak, 2005).

Literature also means a lot as regards the text of Seth's novel; not only the literary allusions within the narrator's or characters discourse, but also the way in which the reading, teaching and study of literature and the performance of drama play an active role in the plot (Rollason, p. 79).

Lata's reading of English Literature at Brahmpur University and later on becoming a Reader in the same department in the 1950s is taken for granted and the value of literary studies as a civilizing influence throughout the world. Gradually, what we find is that the meeting of Lata with Kabir also coincides with his going through the pages of the 'Penguin Book of Contemporary Verse' (a real life anthology); later on, both are seen participating in William Shakespeare's play *Twelfth Night*. In one way or the other, all three suitors of Lata have links with literature. Haresh, the final contender, is an ardent reader of Hardy. Although English, Hindi, Urdu and Bengali have been highlighted by the author, yet the Indian literary tradition is not neglected; we have ample reference to the works of Tagore and also details of the performance of Ramlila in Brahmpur. Hence, in a sense, literature is perceived as a necessary and most vital mode of communication. This theme of communication in *A Suitable Boy* also takes up music as an important means of link. It is found in this work and also in other works of Seth that music appears as a mode of interaction, running parallel to that of language. It is often in the form of the North Indian or Hindustani musical tradition; there is also the presence of the Western tradition of music; that is in the form of performance of Schubert Leider in the Chaterjee family. In fact, the textual gestures point to the world of Seth's later novel *An Equal Music*. Music as a theme of communication revolves round Saeeda Bai, who becomes a subject of admiration and fascination for Maan Kapoor. Communication in any form, be it language, literature or music is the crux of *A Suitable Boy*, Saeeda Bai plays a key role. Gradually, Maan and Firoz become friends, one Hindu and the other a Muslim; their friendship transcends all barriers of religion, culture is perceived in spite of all problems by the reader as an interesting case of secularist and multicultural attitudes. In a way, music was instrumental in starting an affair between Maan and Saeeda Bai, Firoz initiates an affair with Tasneem, who happens to be a close relative of Saeeda Bai. As the story proceeds, the Pul Mela festival coincides with the Shia mourning ceremony of Muharram, and this flares up to a riot. Maan saves Firoz's life, but a small misunderstanding compels him to stab Firoz to death, virtually putting many including Maan's father's political career into trouble. Seth, through his highlighting of this small misunderstanding that leads to big consequences, hints at more efforts required to connect across barriers. This misunderstanding also hints at more problematic Hindu-Muslim interactions. This has always reminded a central theme for all major contemporary Indian writers. Here, we can well compare Vikram Seth with other significant fictional explorations of writers, namely those of Anita Desai, *Clear Light Day*, 1980 or Manju Kapur, *A Married Woman*, 2002 (Rollason, p. 81).

The novel *A Suitable Boy* is Indian and has 'Indianness' as the crux of the story. Although 'Seth has resisted being classified as an Indian writer'; his book 'The Golden Gate' even though has an alien, transatlantic setting but still has received much acclaim from R.K. Narayan as an 'extraordinary work' and 'no small achievement'. If the nineteenth century influence of European fiction is evident on *A Suitable Boy*, this text also points to the ancient Indian epics. There is already reference to Ramlila being performed at Brahmpur, another incident where Pran's mother is seen praying before a calendar from 'Paramahans & Co, Chemists and Druggists', having a picture of Rama, Sita, Laxman and Hanuman with sage Valmiki seated on the ground writing their story on a scroll. Dipankar writes to Amit suggesting similarities between river Ganges and Amit's unfinished novel. Here, Amit may be taken as the alter ego for Vikram Seth. In other words, we can say that Ganga is the possible model for Seth's tale of Brahmpur; there is yet another model from Anglo-Indian fiction, that of R.K. Narayan's Malgudi. Although it is said that Seth ardently followed George Eliot and Thomas Hardy, yet they do not have such devices in any of their novels where we can say that Seth has taken some cue.

V

To conclude, Vikram Seth's novel *A Suitable Boy* is a complex document of the postcolonial reality with its rejection of the Imperial British culture. The text deals with the problems of identity, which includes personal, religious and national issues, through a sequence of contexts. Certain hierarchies are institutionalized and reversed and ultimately they are deconstructed. With the socio-cultural ramifications, the bulk of the text projects a realistic picture of India. There are comprehensive details of Pul Mela, the ordinary life of Rasheed's village, the horror of communal riots and the whole election procedure of campaigning, polling and counting. All these episodes of the novel contribute to a very wide socio-political structure. Several jokes and anecdotes from popular Indian folk tales have been incorporated into the text. The wider spectrum of the socio-cultural forces provides the historical dimension to the lives of the characters. The sequence of events turns between individual attitude and cultural forces. The individual lives are projected as the unconscious working that emerges from the historical forces. India as a nation is reinvented in *A Suitable Boy*. From the point of view of the social history, it presents the picture of life in postcolonial India. The image of the subcontinent is projected so as to reconcile varieties of religions and languages that form the national identity. The identity is revealed in terms of the episodes of the first general election that follows the story of the Partition. The issues that involve the national Indian politics in the period up to the first national election of 1952 are highlighted. The Hindu-Muslim hostilities, the status of the lower class of people, the land reforms and the ending of the era of the feudal princes and landlords. The empowerment of Muslim women and the academic affairs during the post-Independent period are also highlighted in this postcolonial text. The plot of the novel describes the affairs of four families: the Mehras, the Kapoors, the Chatterjees and the Khans. The crisis at the domestic front of these families brings an account of the historical and the social events of the post-Independent era. This is how the plot of the novel appears to be multi-charactered in which the mothers are against the daughters, fathers are against the sons, Hindus against Muslims and small farmers are opposed to greedy landowners. The story moves round Lata Mehra, who is independent-minded. The question remains whether she will defy the rigid decisions of her widowed upper-caste Hindu mother by marrying the Muslim youth whom she loves. In this process, the search for Lata's husband is fitted into the structures of the narrative that is interwoven with the fabric of India. Seth provides a comprehensive and panoramic spectacle that takes us into the law courts, religious processions, bloody riots, and even to the shoe trade. The episodes are set between 1950 and 1952, and this period is characterised by some significant incidents like the rise of the Indian middle class and the consolidation of the Indian states along the secular norms under the administration of Nehru. The private coincides with the public issues of the narrative. All these incidents resolve around the legislation and implementations of land reforms undertaken by the Congress government in the 1950s. In this context, such attempts and explorations of the social, political and economic changes during the initial period after Independence have been made.

The comparison between Salman Rushdie's *Midnight's Children* and Vikram Seth's *A Suitable Boy* throws more light on their approach to the postcolonial reality in their texts. *Midnight's Children* celebrates the split of the polity, because it indicates the pluralism of democracy as opposed to the dictatorial discourse of Mrs Gandhi's regime. On the other hand, the political climate that Vikram Seth signifies is different from that of Emergency. In fact, *A Suitable Boy* provides the impression of a Nehruvian epic. He brings an account of Nehru's faith in secularism, which can suggest the only solution to the complex issues in the Indian scenario, because the minorities like Muslims and people of the lower caste were excluded from the traditional polity. Seth's novel provides a suitable history of post-Partition India and it emphasises the profound issues such as inter-communal relations and the Zamindari system. The challenges for the Congress government after Independence were of greater proportion after defeating the colonial adversary. However, the major steps undertaken by Nehru's government have been highlighted by the novelist with a touch of postcolonial experience.

4 History House as the Backdrop

Roy's *The God of Small Things*

Postcolonial texts like Salman Rushdie's *Midnight's Children* and Arundhati Roy's *The God of Small Things* depict the stories of the struggle against imperialism. These texts also bring out the contradictions inherent in the independence nationalist movement. India was an oppressed nation under the direct control and subjugation of imperialist Britishers. After independence, the national leaders took control of the affairs of their own country, but the postcolonial scenario displayed such incidents and issues which the people did not expect. No doubt the ruling classes were another version of the colonial rulers. The national leaders of the revolt made use of the language of independence and the struggle for freedom to hide their real self. They continued their attacks and exploitation of the working class and the peasant community. Arundhati Roy, in her text, suggests how the marginalized have become victims of the politics of nationalism. Postcolonial literature examines this problem and brings out the effects of decolonization. This is one of the distinguishing themes of the postcolonial literature which projects the subject of nationalism and its failures.

The postcolonialist clings to the nationalist politics of the anti-imperialist struggle. To put it in another way, he still clings to capitalism. In India, the nationalist ruling parties enforce the inhuman caste system, render the country to a police state and relentlessly attack the rebels, the rural working class Arundhati Roy sternly criticises the post-Independent Indian government for its deficiency in fulfilling the needs of the common mass. She elaborately focuses on the national, caste and religious issues and treats the Syrian Christian community as a marginalized section in postcolonial India.

II

Roy's novel shows how globalization and colonialism are interconnected. She brings out the impact of globalization and colonialism on India. As a postcolonial text, *The God of Small Things* presents the idea of how India as a nation is shaped by globalization and colonial policies. Arundhati Roy raises a pertinent question: 'is globalization about the eradication of world poverty or is it a mutant variety of colonialism, remote controlled and digitally operated?' Thus, such issues as India's economy and the Indian diaspora are presented in the novel. It also suggests the way in which caste and colonialist ideals have greater impact on the emergence of identity during the time of globalization. In one sense, India's colonial history cannot be ignored, because it has given rise to complex issues of the postcolonial society. For example, the British East India Company started its operations in 1600 exclusively for commercial purposes. But subsequently, it became an instrument of colonial rule and power. So, the connection with the global market was structured long before India's independence in 1947.

In fact, postcolonial theory concentrates on the issue of power, economies, politics and culture. Moreover, it shows how these components function in relation to colonial hegemony. In Roy's *The God of Small Things*, there has been an attempt to examine the link between colonization and decolonization. At the same time, the novel brings out the process of globalization and its link with post-Independence. She presents the impact of global economy or global culture on a province like Kerala. Ultimately, she presents the distinctive effects of globalization. In the beginning of the text, she brings out a commentary on globalization, when Estha walks around Ayemenem. The same chapter indicates the impact of globalization on Ayemenem's waterways and how it has totally changed the life of Rahel's family. The following lines also bring out the impact of globalization on the life of Baby Kochamma:

It wasn't something that happened overnight … . They stayed at the same hotel. And in Ayemenem, where over the loudest … picturesque massacres and Bill Clinton could be summoned up like servants. And so, … . Baby Kochamma followed American NBA league games … tournaments. On weekdays … . Santa Barbara … . Baby Kochamma loved their shiny clothes and the smart, bitchy repartee. During the day disconnected snatches of it came back to her and made her chuckle. Kochu Maria, the cook, still wore the thick gold earrings that had disfigured her earlobes forever. She enjoyed the WWF Wrestling Mania shows, where Hulk Hogan and Mr Perfect, whose necks were wider than their heads, were spangled Luca leggings and beat each other up brutally. Kochu Maria's language had that slightly cruel ring to it that young children sometimes have.

All day they sat in the drawing room, Baby Kochamma on the long-armed planter's chair or the chaise longue (depending on the condition of her feet), Kochu Maria next to her on the floor (channel surfing when she could), locked together in a noisy television silence. One's hair snow white, the other's dyed coal black. They entered all the contests, availed themselves of all the discounts that were advertised and had, on two occasions, won a T-shirt and a thermos flask that Baby Kochamma kept locked in her cupboard.

Baby Kochamma loved the Ayemenem house and cherished the furniture that she had inherited by outliving everybody else. Mammachi's violin and violin stand, the Ooty cupboards, the plastic basket chairs, the Delhi beds, the dressing table from Vienna with cracked ivory knobs. The rosewood dining table that Velutha made. She was frightened by the BBC famines and television wars that she encountered while she channel-surfed. Her old fear of the

Revolution and the Marxist-Leninist menace had been rekindled by new television worries about the growing numbers of desperate and dispossessed people. She viewed ethnic cleansing, famine and genocide as direct threats to her furniture. Instead of taking care of her garden, she is deeply engrossed in watching satellite television in her drawing room.

This is how Arundhati Roy presents a historical treatment of colonization, decolonization and postcolonialism with the historical backdrop of globalization. There are some areas which bring out the idea of terror that Rahel's family experiences. This is obviously linked to the history of British colonization and to the new phenomenon of globalization. This recent trend has made the Indians at Cochin airport despise themselves. This is how Arundhati Roy's novel presents the idea of globalization as a composition of both colonial rule and postcolonialism.

III

The discourse of marginality is one of the distinguishing features of postcolonial literature. 'Marginality,' says Ashcroft, 'is the condition constructed by the posited relation to a privileged centre' (Ashcroft et al., 2002: 102) (Prasad, 2006: 157). The postcolonial condition of the characters in the novel is manifested in the issue that concerns marginality. The novel presents the aspects of socialism and feminism and the postcolonial conditions suggested by putting forth the limitation of being an untouchable or a woman. Marginality is represented by such characters as Velutha, Ammu, Rahel and Estha. They are the small things and protagonists of the story. They occupy a peripheral position either in their family or in the framework of the society. In this sense, *The God of Small Things* incorporates such themes as marriage, divorce, separation, abuse, alienation and death. The text raises the issue of gender, class division, political and religious conflicts. Marginality that which is based on gender, class oppression, cultural difference or differential experiences of powerlessness has shaped the content of a flourishing range of recent postcolonial narratives (ibid.).

The picturization of the dispossessed and exploited groups seems to form a kind of interconnection or bond among themselves. They point towards the cultural realities compounded of such ingredients as deprivation, desperation, moral entropy and hypocrisy in the social and the so-called material practices of the postcolonial arena. Bill Ashcroft says '[b]y appropriating strategies of representation, organisation and social changes through access to global system, local communities and marginal interest groups can both empower themselves and influence those global systems' [Ashcroft, 2006, n. pag (online)]. *The God of Small Things* is a writing of resistance where the subaltern section has been represented. Nagesh Rao says Roy in her discourse has a postcolonial nation as both 'the material referent' and 'the condition of production' [Rao, 2004, n. pag (online)].

The novel of Arundhati Roy is an intersection of many discourses and marginality like feminism, caste segregation and untouchability. Roy has projected in her writings the conflict between power and powerlessness. The novel is one that deals with the subaltern groups and individuals, the oppressed and marginalized class of people. This is highlighted by a confined and constricted woman who is contained by her pains and sufferings, her children dislodged and a low-caste skilled carpenter up against the norms of the society and power. The story of the novel is the story of Ammu's marginalization and Velutha's silence surrounded by the absence of power, and the absence of self-determination. The use of language in the novel is such that it constructs and helps dissolve the strong and rigid ideological structures. These structures have been historically woven into the 'smell' victims and sustained marginalization. Further in the novel, Roy suggests a clear connection between narrative strategies and the oppressive fetters, the socio-historical realities that the protagonist has to contend against. *The God of Small Things* also highlights in more than one way the subjugation of the woman folk represented by Ammu by the traditional male authority. The text enhances the sense of marginality among its characters. Ammu, sister of Chacko, is a major character in the novel. She decides to marry a man of her choice, a Bengali-Hindu who is an assistant manager in a tea-estate in Assam; this very act of her is something 'un-Christian'. She acts against those who are in command of the Ayemenem house, but her transformation was almost doomed from the very beginning. She is divorced and returns to the Ayemenem house with her twins. Here, the illegal is made legal by her act of having an affair with the untouchable Velutha. This affair with a Paravan constitutes a transgression. Ammu's relationship with Velutha leads to tragedy that leaves her twins Rahel and Estha 'doomed waifs' with a precarious life and away from her.

Velutha is placed by the author at the periphery of the caste-ridden, feudal Ayemenem house; his name suggests ('white'), quite a symbolic link of blackness with dirt, and white with that of purity is just a kind of reversal with his representation. According to Tabish Khair, who puts it in a different context altogether, his body 'exceeds subalternity' (Khair, 2000: 14); he states that his body is poised in opposition to hegemonic control.

Arundhati Roy has also tried to project the issue of 'subdued biology' (Roy, 1997: 107). This happens to be the main concern in the novel *The God of Small Things*. The term 'biology' is used metaphorically to highlight the union with nature for the lovers; it is a kind of attraction that gives them the momentum to transform the social dispositions. The concern of the author is highlighted in chapter 11 'The God of Small Things' Ammu's 'subdued biology'. It was not what lay at the end of her road that frightened Ammu as much as the nature of the road itself. No milestones marked its progress. No trees grew along it. No dappled shadows shaded it. No mist rolled over it. No birds circled it. No twists, no turns or hairpin bends obscured even momentarily, her clear view of the end. This filled Ammu with an awful deed because she wasn't the kind of woman who wanted her future told … . And what Ammu knew … smelled of the vapid, vinegary fumes that rose from the cement vats of Paradise Pickles. Fumes that wrinkled youth and pickled futures. Hooded against her own hair, Ammu leaned against herself in the bathroom mirror and tried to weep.

For herself.
For the God of Small Things.
For the sugar-dusted twin midwives of her dreams. (224)

The phrase *The God of Small Things* sums up all the impressive transactions in this text. According to M.K. Naik, 'It is Velutha who gives the novel its title. 'The God of Small Things. It is he who is that kind of a god' (2003: 66).

Although Velutha has the outstanding gifts of manual dexterity, skills, humour, ingenuity and the power to overcome social inequalities, he remains a Paravan by birth. According to Devon Campbell-Hall:

> Although Velutha has control of the entire process of manufacturing his creations, his lack of caste status prevents the empowerment usually associated with the real artisan. Certainly he enjoys far more social freedom than most skilled labourers of his social status, but Roy's is a bitter critique of the hypocrisy of the fictional Syrian Christian world. In her native Kerala, this clearly highlights her frustration with the injustice of an ancient caste system that condemns certain citizens to lives of drudgery simply because of an accident of birth. Roy's representation of Velutha as an artisan pushing against the restrictive boundaries challenges not only the traditional caste distinction but also postmodern distinctions of globalized class system and systems of production. (Campbell-Hall, 2002–3: 52–53)

The God of Small Things highlights Roy's concern for the people on the margins; themes like women's marginalization, patriarchal authority, feudal survival, state-sponsored terrorism, displacement of masses, oppressive fetters and caste system all clubbed together into one becomes the palpable substance of concern.

IV

The concept of hybridity as developed in *The God of Small Things* is relevant to its postcolonial study. But when there is a discussion with regard to hybridity, obviously issues such as migration and return are to be raised. The consequence of migrating is the composition of hybrid identities, when the migrants interact with the local population. From a biological point of view, a hybrid is an offspring with parents, who belong to different races. In this sense, Sophie Mol is the only hybrid in this novel, because her father is an Indian and her mother Margaret is an English woman. Another form of hybridity is pointed out by Baby Kochamma herself: 'Baby Kochamma disliked the twins, for she considered them doomed, fatherless waifs. Worse still, they were Half-Hindu Hybrids whom no self-respecting Syrian Christian would ever marry' (45). She calls the twins hybrid in connection with their religion, because their father Baba is Hindu and their mother Ammu is a Syrian Christian.

In her essay 'Language, Hybridity and Dialogism in *The God of Small Things'*, Anna Clarke explains why discussion with regard to hybridity is relevant to postcolonialism: 'hybridity as a critical concept has had a privileged place in postcolonial studies. This is because contact and intermixture between different cultural groups have taken place in the historical context of colonization.'

Since colonial relationships were relationships of power between what the colonizers saw as the privileged 'enlightened', 'civilized', 'rational', and 'advanced', colonizers and the subaltern 'barbaric', 'superstitious', 'backward', colonized, hybridity in such contexts has often taken on a politicised dimension (Clarke, 2007: 138).

In his celebrated work *The Location of Culture*, Homi Bhabha looks for the space where culture can actually be found. Anna Clarke explains this, 'To put it simply, the location of the meaning of culture is the contact zone between cultures; the space of culture's hybridity' (Bhabha, 1994: 138). Homi Bhabha calls this space the 'Third Space', in addition to the first two spaces or the two separate sides. Actually, it depends on the hybrid himself to define exactly what the third space looks like or where it is. In *The God of Small Things*, Chacko says, 'We belong nowhere, we sail unanchored on troubled seas. We may never be allowed ashore'

(53), Salman Rushdie had a similar idea in *Imaginary Homelands:* 'Our identity is at once plural and partial. Sometimes we feel that we straddle two cultures, at other times that we fall between two stools' (Rushdie, 1991: 15). In *The God of Small Things*, this is particularly applied to Chacko, because he has lived through English habits and cultures and at the same time, he also follows the Indian moral values.

Hybridity happens to be the most important theme of the novel. This hybridity of the twins later in the novel becomes instrumental in leading the tragedy of the twins and their mother. The interreligious marriage of Ammu degrades the twins, whereas the same logic does not apply for Sophie Mol, who is the issue of interracial marriage of Chacko and Margaret. Ammu's relationship with Velutha develops all possibilities of yet another hybrid child. Velutha is an untouchable and therefore his association with Ammu is perceived as a real threat to the social order. The twins though belong to a higher caste are still considered as inferior because the Indian system does not completely recognise it. Estha and Rahel's case does not apply to Sophie Mol, Chacko's own daughter. Both Ammu and Chacko had defied social order by marrying out of their own caste or group but had to pay a heavy price by the collapse of their married life. It is often found that a woman's labour is always rewarded by loss. This is the case with Ammu because she was deprived of any share in her parents' factory. This is true with all divorcees and more so with someone who has married by her own initiative. Ammu, the main character, lives on sufferings with her children. 'Tell your mother to take you to your father's house,' she said. 'There you can break as many beds as you like. These aren't your beds. This isn't your house,' (83) she has to face and hear all this in spite of her hard work at the pickles factory. 'Though Ammu did as much work as Chacko, whenever he was dealing with food inspectors or sanitary engineers, he always referred to it as my factory, my pineapples, my pickles. Legally, this was the case, because Ammu, as a daughter, had no claim to the property (57). Hybridity also affects another person whom Ammu terms 'God of Small Loss'. Velutha is enfeebled by the symbol of power (police) for two reasons, firstly for jealousy and for having sex with a woman of high-caste, this is what roused discussions in the society. The relationship of Velutha was a mere potentiality of a hybrid child; 'And a history lesson for future offenders' (336). This offence is in accordance with the hatred, the feared or the despised Other. Homi Bhabha has rightly remarked:

> The paranoid thrust from the hybrid is finally uncontainable because it breaks down the symmetry and duality of self/other, inside/outside. The untouchables are always placed at the periphery. The upper-caste families always guard themselves and their houses which are away from the reach of those untouchables. The attitude of the people towards caste system is rigid as these untouchables have a separate church from that of the higher classes. 'When the British came to Malabar, a member of the Paravans, Pethyas and Pulayas (among them Velutha's grandfather, Kelan) converted to Christianity and joined the Anglican Church to escape the scourge of Untouchability'.

As added incentive they were given a little food and also money. They were known as the Rice-Christians. It didn't take them long to realise that they had jumped from the frying pan into the fire. They were made to have separate churches, with separate services, and separate priests. As a special favour, they were given their own separate Pariah Bishop (74). In the novel, we find a display of hypocrisy on the part of the people, including Mammachi herself; when she allows Velutha to enter her house to fix up something. There are instances when orthodox Brahmins though employ Untouchables to work and also sprinke water over their dishes which the Untouchable servant had cleaned. Arundhati Roy very aptly through images places the high-caste family on the same platform as the Paravan. Velutha is the Paravan who was killed for having 'entered' a forbidden place. Chacko faced the same failure as his father Pappachi, who had struggled to get recognized by the English for his discovery of the moth and thus also failed to get a promotion. Chacko also failed on another count – he could not establish himself in society as a good businessman as he had no contribution in keeping the factory going. It was Ammu and the other two women, Mammachi and Baby Kochamma, who had given their part for the factory. It is therefore found that hybridity has on many occasions pulled down the characters of the novel.

V

The God of Small Things is written on a particular locale named Ayemenem. It is the ancestral place of Ammu or the matriarchal place of Rahel and Estha, the zygotic twins. The novel is to some extent at par with Rushdie's *Midnight's Children* 'as one enters the magical world of *The God of Small Things*, the powerful poetic, prose elevates one's senses (Balvannandhan, 2007).

Rahel, the chief narrator or protagonist, guides through the narration to trudge along the final stages of the ordeal behind the History House. The Ayemenem House is called the History House. It can be said that gradually all the characters of history are caught in the clutches of history. The story progresses through different phases where we find the notion of hybridity with the twins and the relationship of Ammu with Velutha. It all develops in a postcolonial setup where a group from the society is leading a colonized life within a postcolonial perspective.

Chacko represents the colonial forces as he considers himself as having everything foreign, particularly his Plymouth car and his wife Margaret. Chacko, being the representative of the colonial forces, is free to sexually exploit the women workers. On the other hand, the marriage of Ammu is looked down upon, including her relations with Velutha. The whole novel is set against the backdrop of Kerala, which happens to be one of the smallest states of India, formed in 1956. It was the first state in India to have a democratically elected Communist government in 1957. It was in 1969 that Kerala witnessed demonstrations; the period between 1957 and 1970 is rightly described by Roy as not quite palatable. There was a deep caste divide and the death of Communist leader and the creator of the Naxalbari Movement, Charu Mazumdar, also created disturbance to a certain extent in 1972.

Before the coming of the British to India, the position of women was much higher, but after the colonial interference and changing of certain laws the matriarchal Hindu society changed considerably as it was unacceptable to the colonial powers. It was in spite of all loud avowals that there was open interference by the Imperial power in the affairs of the society, and the women were still further reduced to a status of a nonentity. This process started in 1868 and continued well into the 1930s. The form of family organization gave the women the economic power and sexual freedom. With regard to the Marriage Commission, the right to terminate any union at any time from wantonness or caprice was brought to a controlled framework. The same colonial interference influenced the cultural life in India. During the period, the nationalists of the time were not promoting Victorian values.

The British were also a step ahead in erasing the practice by women to dance in temples, women's writing also went against the wishes of the British, and hence they also underwent Victorian censure. The Kerala that has been projected in the novel by Arundhati Roy has in fact regressed in many aspects, because before the British intervention the same women enjoyed more freedom and legal rights. When we go into the narration, we find that hybridity is a major cause of suffering for the twins as well as their mother. The position of the twins is lowered as their mother marries an Untouchable. It is seen in the book of Hindu precepts entitled the 'Manavadharmashastra' that when a man marries a lower caste woman, he elevates her status. But if a woman does it, she loses her caste. Here, there is a possibility of another hybrid child with the relationship of Ammu with Velutha. Chacko, on the other hand, has had an inter-racial marriage and this poses no problem either for him or for Sophie Mol. But the inter-caste marriage of Ammu and Velutha creates a sense of isolation for herself as well as the children, who are isolated because they are hybrid by birth. They are brown and therefore need to be separated from the white race. It is within the family that the children feel the anxiety between the reality of the family and their position in society in the historical context. They feel that they are caste-offs of history in regard to India's colonial past.

Though the twins are from a high-caste family, they suffer due to their inferior breed which the Indian system does not accept. Sophie Mol is also hybrid, same as Estha and Rahel, but she is a product of two systems – race and class. Defiance of the social order was committed by both Ammu as well as Chacko by marrying out of their own caste or group. Study has revealed that there is an existent division between races – blacks and whites. Transgression of this division was in the case of Chacko and Margaret. But with regard to religion or community, it was manifested in the case of Ammu and her husband. As discussed by critics, hybridity plays an important role in this novel, this has also affected the interaction between the West and the East, and its outcome is always negative.

In this novel, religion and caste also play an important role in the shaping of things. Religion has been the basis of human savagery and intolerance; however, this has been rejected throughout the novel. Velutha has been compared to Jesus throughout the novel and is finally murdered and registered in official history. The children Estha and Rahel have always defended the Dalits. Velutha is presented as a *God of Small Things* (330).

In order to delve deeply into the novel, we may consider the background of the caste system in India. The caste system has been since ages an integral part of the Hindu tradition. To be a bit more precise, it dates back to 1200 BC, and was first used by the Portuguese, who came to India in the sixteenth century. The word 'caste' is derived from the Spanish and Portuguese, word 'casta', which means 'race', 'breed', or 'linage'. The Indian caste system was divided according to their profession into four classes. They are The Brahmans, The Kshatriyas, The Vaishyas, and The Sudras. The caste of any particular person not only demarcates one's occupation but diet as well as his or her interaction with members of other castes. The Untouchables are outside the caste gamut, they perform the lowliest of jobs in the society. Hence, they are considered to be in the permanent state of impurity.

Although the laws regarding various factors to govern the society were framed since ages, in *The God of Small Things,* the laws of India's caste system have been defied by characters such as Ammu and Velutha. He is an Untouchable Paravan, working in Paradise Pickles and Preserves. He was a bit outspoken and gave suggestions even if not asked for. He was resented by the other workers and was also paid less. He was a kind of an unwanted guest wherever he went, he was also disliked because of the way in which he disregarded suggestions without appearing to rebel (73).

The ancient Hindu belief maintains that being an Untouchable is a punishment. Untouchability is a curse in Indian society. Although Velutha was a dedicated Communist party worker, yet he was quite disliked by his party members just for his inferior status. Velutha in spite of having all the drawbacks had an affair with Ammu. He breaks the age-old tradition and taboo of the society and thereby incurs the wrath of the family of Ammu and also the Kerala police. The policemen act out of fear Civilization's – fear, fear of nature, men's fear of women, fear of powerless (*The God of Small Things,* p. 292). In the Keralite society, there is a wide gap between the so-called touchable and the Untouchables. In the novel, Roy projects the dangerous effects of industrialization. The whole novel is a search for the essence of life, truth, in a totally corrupt and degenerated world where capitalism has taken the shape of globalization. This novel is also a kind of lesson for the people, that the lust for power is the key factor for the destruction of people who do not succumb to the dominant authorities. In a way, they do not submit to the established dominant rules and instead, live in accordance with nature.

History happens to be central; it is also called the supreme fiction, which is as a rule to be recreated in a continuous process of sequences. History must suggest to people that they can write their past, the novel enters into history and also history enters into the novel. It also states that there is no human condition, which is outside the preview of history or society. Critics also say that in women's writing, we find a perfect combination of history, community and fiction, and it owes its origin to fictional autobiography or autobiographical fiction.

In Arundhati Roy's fiction, there is no autobiography but there is plain resemblance to her lost past. There is history recreated through fiction. Roy has fictionalized her past, which is history; but the process is also quite painful, so there is also pain and reality in the fiction.

Any autobiographical novel gives its author a chance 'to reassess his or her past and to reinterpret a plethora of racial, sexual and cultural codes inscribed on personal consciousness ... transforming experience through fiction.' In this novel, many things take place. Estha has come back to Ayemenem after a long, long time, and is finding it difficult to adjust. Ammu has failed to accept the social dictum that a boy needs a 'Baba' (31); this becomes instrumental in their separation instead of keeping them together. Society also plays an important role in creating 'Edges, Borders, Boundaries, Brinks, Limits', which appear like a group of social blockades which are quite difficult to crossover; as adults, they enter into a kind of confusion about their own identity, and at the same time a common inability to come to terms with any meaningful relationships. They had to face all these only because of their hybridity and their mother's divorce; they were also deprived of all the ancestral claims. As a matter of convention, the children of a divorced daughter had no position in society, they are not accepted in the patriarchal society, as a divorced daughter had no place anywhere.

The children's only sign of social identity is also uncertain (surname) as their mother is also quite not sure about that. She too does not have much of a choice. The relationship they see and also experience and for that matter every relationship in history has been flawed, unhappy and doomed. Hence, there is little room for them to enter into a relationship with the hope of fulfilment. The situation that has developed with the uncertainties and their struggle for a meaningful existence are nothing but an image and objective correlative for a society which is struggling on the edge of splitting apart. The conventionally middle-class values combine with the newly-born communism. In this world, the educated and well-born women are marginalised and the powerless agree in their own suffering and participate unconditionally in the power of the oppressor. The novel is a narration of a story that transcends time and scope. It is the story of the world since the beginning of the society. Indian Marxism has branded this novel as an insult to the Communists and Communism of Kerala. They fail to get the true spirit of the novel. This novel in a way has a kind of antipathy towards the Marxists and it does not make itself called a political novel. Hence, 'no discourse can be politically neutral from this point of view'. Human relationships are everywhere, within fiction or without, based on a struggle for power, a class struggle. The conflicting identities are always oppressors and victims. Certainly, Ammu, Rahel, Estha and Velutha are victims because they are powerless.

According to Antonia Navarro Tejaro, Arundhati Roy in *The God of Small Things* has written against globalization. It shows the way in which it generates corruption, goes against truth, and how capitalism takes centre-stage in a degenerated world. She has clearly highlighted how hypocrisy and lust for power crush people who choose not to submit to established and dominant norms. Personal stories that Roy narrates question the power structures. She also makes an ardent attempt to change them through the power of literature.

The novel focuses on the binary 'house/factory', representing the 'inside/outside' dichotomy. It also focuses on its people who are equally in power relationships. The novel also investigates how the powerless are oppressed by the powerful, the 'Big' three power structures: Family, State, and Religion. All these three power structures are the epitomes to which people look up to, but these have been degenerated by the feelings of power and control. The story has focussed on the significance of the factory. It is not a simple place, but a place from where Communism sprang up, a place which allows rebellion to start. Here we find the fall of domestic business, modernization and capitalism taking over, Dalits being exploited, and women being sexually abused. It is also found in this novel how some male characters associate themselves with Marxist ideologies. They are seen having alliance with capitalism and thereby being instrumental in ruining the life of the chief protagonist. The idea that Karl Marx propounded was that capitalism is a conspiracy by the powerful class of the society against those who are powerless.

Chacko is a very important character of the novel. He is a self-styled Communist, who left his job just to run his mother's pickles factory. He made all sorts of charity like helping the poor and the needy whenever he came to know of their problems. Chacko, although proclaims himself to be a Communist, hardly follows the ideals of Marx. Instead, he becomes one of the exploiters of the powerless.

There are three categories of women around the factory, one being displaced like Mammachi and the other dispossessed like that of Ammu, the third, sexually abused or exploited, like the factory workers.

Chacko was sent to Oxford to complete his studies; there he fell in love with a girl named Margaret, who later becomes the mother of Chacko's daughter. But, Margaret divorces Chacko and marries an Englishman. Gradually, the story takes a turn. Chacko returns to India, takes up the job of teaching. He joins Madras Christian College as a Reader. He gets to know the difference between his Communist ideals and his working in an institute which is allied to a religious entity. The death of Pappachi is yet another turning point in the story. He resigns and goes to Ayemenem to take over the family business:

> 'with his Balliol Oar and his Pickles Baron dreams' (54). The whole episode of Chacko taking over the family business from his mother implies that the society is male dominant. A woman, howsoever capable, cannot be taken for granted that she will succeed, here it is the widow of his father Pappachi. Mammachi is a victim of displacement within her family, she was displaced from

> the family business by her own son; highlighting the fact that this is a gender-biased society. Chacko 'had it registered as a partnership and informed Mammachi that she was a sleeping partner' (57). Capitalist ideas taking over are quite evident from the fact when Chacko proceeds to 'modernise', goes ahead to make it a capitalist enterprise and also gave it a name. This modernisation drive of Chacko pushed the factory to the brink of bankruptcy. This is clear-cut evidence as to how money operated in factories and what its power is and to what extent it was responsible for the degeneration of the family.

Chacko named the factory 'Paradise Pickles and Preserves'. The name 'Paradise' is quite ironic in this context. By going for a new name, Chacko had all the doors closed for Mammachi, as she had no say in this matter. It was with comrade K.N.M. Pillai that Chacko discussed the names. After voting out the names like 'Zeus Pickles and Preserves' and 'Parshuram Pickles and Preserves', they finally settled for 'Paradise Pickles and Preserves'. According to them, the word 'Paradise' shall change the town into a modern industrial town. But the name did not stand as conceived, because it was no 'Paradise' for the powerless like the Dalits as it was a complete setting for the exploitation of women.

According to Gayle Rubin, who argues in her book *The Traffic in Women: Notes on the 'Political Economy' of Sex*, that 'if sexism were the by-product of capitalism's relentless appetite for profit, then sexism would wither away in the advent of a successful socialist revolution' (Rubin, 1975: 157).

The factory is a symbol of exploitation of the powerless, especially the women. Arundhati Roy has in strong words denounced women's deprivation. The most important example of this kind of deprivation is Ammu. Although she works as much as Chacko in the factory, she has no say or claim on the property. Chacko declares time and again that anything related to the factory is 'his'. He also tells Ammu that 'what is yours is mine and what's mine is also mine' (57). Rubin further writes in her book 'that capitalism is just an heir to a long tradition in which women do not inherit, in which women do not lead, and in which women do not talk to god' (164). In the novel, Arundhati Roy has exposed the communist idea. It was when the family wanted to join a protest march while on their way to Cochin that Chacko ordered to roll up all the windows even though they belonged to the same party as he was; 'stay calm, they're not going to harm us'(64). Ammu quickly responded to it, by saying, 'how he could possibly know that in this old car there beats a truly Marxist heart' (70). The protest march was to make sure 'that women's wages be increased from one rupee twenty paisa a day, to three rupees, and men's from two rupees fifty paisa to four rupees fifty paisa a day. They were also demanding that the Untouchables no longer be addressed by their caste names' (69). Chacko called himself a Communist and he perpetuated the established unfair means by two ways, either by gender bias or by discriminating against the Dalits.

In *The God of Small Things*, Arundhati Roy has projected the unfair means of highlighting women as a cheap labour force for the capitalist market, because lower wages provide extra surplus to a capitalist employer. Chacko although proclaims himself to be a Communist, yet projected as a manipulator of ideas. He calls women to his room and forces his lust on them on the pretext of giving them lectures on labour rights and trade union laws:

> '... [A] landlord forcing attentions on women who depended on him for their livelihood'. (65)
>
> Chacko has a different version of himself. He is described as a recreation of the old traditional landlord with an English influence, because he got the advantage (by force) of being the owner. Thus, he behaved as a feudal landlord. Ammu called him 'case of a spoiled prince-ling playing comrade! comrade! An Oxford avatar, of the old zamindars' mentality'. (65)

Silent support was extended for Chacko and his outrageous demands on the women workers of the factory. Even Mammachi and Baby Kochamma did not find any difference between Chacko's Marxist ideals and the feudal libido or the psychic instinct for sex. She had another entrance built for the women workers to go and come into Chacko's room. Mammachi instead made efforts to separate needs from feelings and she was able to manage the situation by giving money, 'they took it because they needed it, they had young children and old parents, or husbands who spent all their earnings in toddy bars' (169). But Mammachi and Baby Kochamma had different feelings for the Naxalites, 'who had been known to force men from good families to marry servant girls whom they had made pregnant' (168).

In *The God of Small Things*, Arundhati Roy has brought out a crucial difference between Chacko and Ammu. Chacko is always seen as one of the exploiters of female sexuality, whereas Ammu is sexually exploited. Chacko's improper advances towards the factory workers are tolerated and the juxtaposing of this act with Ammu's love affair with Velutha is horrendously repulsive to Mammachi (*The God of Small Things*, p. 257). According to Arundhati Roy, this in a way has highlighted the male-dominated society and its misdoings. The society that has been projected in the novel highlights how the patriarchal social norms have been given importance by the first generation of women and to what extent they surrender themselves to it. Even the woman from high class society (Ammu) is not an exception to this system and the situation became unbearable to the whole traditional conservative community. At home, Mammachi was furious because she had to give sanction to her son's 'Men's Needs' and out poured her anger on her daughter:

> '[Mammachi's] tolerance of 'Men's Needs' as far as her son was concerned, became the fuel for her unmanageable fury at her daughter. [...] For generations to come, forever now, people would point at them at weddings and funerals. At baptisms and birthday parties. They'd nudge and whisper. It was all finished now' (*The God of Small Things*, p. 258). Here the whole content of the statement is about division of class and caste which leads to alienation.

The overall situation of the factory is that all the workers are kept within their limits. The women workers are paid less for their labour, but get extra money for 'forced' sexual relations. The Dalits are also kept within their limits. Velutha being a member of the Dalits community is a matter of concern because he also happens to be a card holder of the Communist Party. Further, he is also a skilled carpenter and quite indispensible for the factory. The matter of concern is again connected with power and position. Chacko and comrade K.N.M. Pillai are quite apprehensive of Velutha's association with the party or else they shall face danger from him. Pillai smells danger and asks Chacko to send Velutha away, because his 'Untouchable' condition may create antagonism within the factory workers. Mammachi intervenes and solves the problem suggesting that Velutha should be paid less than a 'Touchable Carpenter'. Still, he is indispensible and skilled. Mammachi always considers that Velutha 'ought to be grateful that he is allowed to touch things that Touchables touched' (77). Here, we again find a caste/class distinction which surfaces in the novel.

Things took a different turn for Velutha when he was falsely accused of killing Sophie Mol and raping Ammu. As a member of the party, he looks up to comrade K.N.M. Pillai, for protection. But, he is insulted by Pillai, a surprised and dazed Velutha becomes speechless. Pillai says 'it is not in the party's interests to take up such matters. Individual's interest is subordinate to the organization's interests. Violating Party Discipline means violating Party Unity' (287). He calls him a 'Comprador Capitalist', and Velutha is left alone, persecuted and feeling that 'another religion turned against itself. Another edifice constructed by the human mind, decimated by human nature' (287).

The projected scenario is a false picture of the goals of Communism. In another sense, we can say that the factory run by a self-proclaimed Communist is a place of oppression for the weak, the downtrodden and the other sex. Actually, no such paradise has been created and those who need real protection are left aside. Rather, the reference to paradise provokes the image of hell and even death, class division and caste division. There is a clear class/master distinction even within the Communist Party and there is a re-play of the power structure. In the end, the factory is projected as a place where the 'lonely drummer drummed. A gauze door slammed. A mouse rushed across the factory floor. Cobwebs sealed old pickle vats. Bone dust from a Bar Nowl. Long dead Pickledowl' (328).

The novel projects the idea of being dispossessed. Baby Kochamma rejects the idea of love and human relationship of any kind. That is the reason why *The God of Small Things* is a timeless, universal tale of the battle between the community and the individual. Hence, the setting is quite appropriate for the climax of the story of Rahel and Estha. This is enacted in the deserted mansion that the children refer to as the 'History House' (History, Community and Forbidden Relationships, p. 88). This History House is now the centre of a dispute, which originally belonged to an English man. Chacko was the one who had told the children that history is like an old house at night, with all its lamps lit. The History House is full of history with a lot of whisper from within which the children and their mother could not understand. The children enter the History House and suddenly things come alive. History reveals itself from the back verandha. According to Chacko, society collapsed only because people forgot their history. He allowed his sense of loss to turn him into a 'monster'. He exhibited what the powerful or the colonizers did with the colonized, or the powerless. He destroyed the children and their mother.

Gradually, things have changed and people have lost their self, transformed to different personalities altogether, Chacko, the uncle, has changed to Chacko, the father, Ammu the mother to Ammu the lover, Estha becomes Brutus and Velutha turns to Christ. The carpenter explains to the children the meaning of love and to their mother the meaning of life. Finally, he is the one who is sacrificed to appease the fear of social and political subversion. It was after the return of Rahel that things started to come back to life. The buried history, personal and social, springs back to life. Past and present co-exist and interpenetrate. The story of Rahel has a dominant tone and a viewpoint, but it's not the only one, because the story is linked to everyone else through a common centre of destructive relationship that defies the social order of the community. The stories are all linked to each other in which history is not in sequence but is repetitive. According to T.S. Eliot, history is 'a pattern of timeless moments'. In a particular pattern, something happens to an individual and it is also applicable to all others in life who live in time. The protagonists represent the community on the one hand and human relationship on the other. There is a difference in the acceptance of the rejection of the objective reality; in postmodernist novel, the same element suggests the fragmentation of the self. In the African women novels, 'it also establishes a communal storyteller-listener relationship through its approximation to the disjointed conversation of everyday life. In *The God of Small Things*, the shifts recreate the arbitrary flights of memory, enact the sundering of familial and social bonds and the dislocation of the quest for selfhood'.

The story of the novel ends in Ammu and Velutha, the two elements of forbidden relationships in the reverse order. They both become an image of the other. There is a reversal of the convectional order of narration. It is quite evident that the present can only lead to the past and the future replicates the past. According to Borges, 'the central problem of the novel is casualty' (qtd in Zaraffa, p. 14). Forbidden relationships are the only media to achieve selfhood for the oppressed, the deprived and the powerless. Marriage plays an important role as a loveless entrepreneurship. After her marriage, Ammu takes a divorce from her husband who is an alcoholic and she returns to Ayemenem but is not welcomed by her parents, especially by her father who was disapproving even during her marriage and also at the time of her divorce.

This highlights that Ammu has no place of her own, no identity and she has no chance of happiness. This was one of the striking reasons why she choose to have a Paravan for her lover, a man who is unacceptable in society, but this man was able to give her all that she thought she had lost. According to Pratt, Velutha symbolises the green lover, an agent of rebirth and of transformation (140). He was kind of a small, sunny meadow on Ammu's Road to Age and Death (337). Velutha was a symbol of wholeness, the relationship between him and Ammu broke all the ancient social and economic barriers of caste and class; Velutha with a leaf shaped mark on his back appears to be a Christ-like figure of regeneration, but he is not at all a sexual outlet for an abandoned Ammu. He shows what love is and how love can bring back to life her inner soul. Hence, he proved himself to be a true partner, which her previous husband could never become for her. Velutha proved to be a fatherly figure for the children. Ammu feels secure when with him as for these reasons.

Rahel, the chief protagonist of the novel, is no exception. She has also had a loveless marriage, she has to choose a husband outside her community; but it is socially accepted, as it conformed to the rules of patriarchy. Still, he does not contribute in any manner to explore the inner feelings and passions, which provides ample ground for Rahel to seek her past. The twins lived in a world where the socially accepted forms of love remain only form without having any substance. Therefore, true love finds expression only in an unacceptable relationship, as in the case of their mother Ammu. Estha reminds of his past, his childhood when he was traumatised by sexual abuse. Rahel also feels for Estha and as twins, they feel for each other. They experience the horror and feel the brutality of the community. Estha finds incest inevitable to find solace from the past experiences but incest happens to be the most tabooed of all relationships, whose outcome is tears.

The coming together of Estha and Rahel to experience each other's emotions and passions is something which is quite natural but has been a kind of stigma framed by the society as unnatural, because it is followed by some act quite similar to that of Ammu and Velutha. Incest is a kind of sexual exploitation that is utilized in the novel to dig out the past and is the product of patriarchal self-assertion. Further, the relationship of Rahel and Estha has its own ironic parallel which foreshadows the incestuous love that Mammachi exhibits for Chacko. As regards fulfilment of one's personal desire, incestuous love evolves a kind of class antagonism. More than that, there is sexual jealousy that makes Mammachi believe that Margret Kochamma is just one of the whores whom he utilizes to fulfil his needs. Here, the author has tried to construct a kind of degenerating situation among the members of the family. The same was also felt during the colonial period when things were done to suit the colonizers.

It is felt that the love between Estha and Rahel is quite natural and there is a real need of it. Still, the union between the two is inevitably doomed. It is an expected truth that the ultimate end of the forbidden relationship is through grief and separation. It is also true that even if the world has changed since the Mahabharata or the childhood of Rahel, history seldom changes. There may be any number of changes all round, the History House also may get a facelift to a heritage hotel, but the future or the tomorrow that Velutha has been promised by Ammu and also to her own self at the end of the novel encompasses the entire range of human passions. So, the tomorrow that comes shall only bring quietness and emptiness. The role that Ammu plays in her attempt to rediscover selfhood in defiance of the rules of nature and society leads to the death of Sophie Mol and Velutha. Her ending also accompanies the destruction of her children's childhood, all that she gains is a lesson of history for the future (336); this is the real cost of living. Comrade Pillai is an observer of Rahel, a divorcee who has come home, shares the same fate as her mother. He also looks at Estha, who has been broken by time. Ammu also died through suffering. Here he views things from a different perspective and tries to find a Marxist moral for the situation.

The Christian establishment had started to collapse. The whole thing has been juxtaposed with all that has happened in Kerala to the secular Marxist ideals and above all, it was against the Marxist betrayal of Velutha. It is also projected through the novel that all the various relationships, those that are not based on love, must collapse. Love can have different perspectives, whether it is a love that transcends social boundaries. It may be parental or filial, or it is self-interest masquerading as political method or strategy. It is also proved by time that where this love is forbidden, betrayal of some kind is bound to crop up. There are numerable examples as Brutus betrayed Caesar, Kunti, Karna, Father Mulligan his Christian mission, and Estha, Velutha. It is also projected that the love of Ammu and Velutha is considered as a betrayal of their class loyalties and of conventional notions regarding feminine chastity.

Human relationship is always based on the need and the capacity to reach out to other individuals. As in the case of the colonial forces, they had the need as well as the ability to reach out and then dominate that section of the society where there was slight weakness or a scope to show off or project one's superiority. In *The God of Small Things*, the quest for one's own self is more closely linked to the need for love. Revolt against the system is a sheer act of desperation which is not chosen by instinct and is something that leads to defeat. The death of Ammu is instrumental in bringing about a union though forbidden of Estha and Rahel. As the relationship is forbidden, it is destined to be doomed.

The God of Small Things is a story of lost dreams which can be seen from many points of view. All the characters have something or the other to lose and say about their loss. All the five generations of those that stayed in the Ayemenem house have suffered. Sophie Mol came to stay at Ayemenem house with her mother Margaret Kochamma to live with her real father Chacko. Things changed rapidly and unexpectedly, all within a few days. It is often said by people that things change in a day and a few hours can affect results of a lifetime. When they affect life, those few hours must be picked up from the ruins and examined. Ayemenem house, which is projected by Roy, has a story to tell. 'The description of summer in Ayemenem is something unique: May in Ayemenem is a hot, brooding month. The days are long and humid. The river shrinks and black crows gorge on the bright mangoes in still, dust green trees. Red bananas ripen. Jackfruit burst.' These lines replicate the history of India, all that was a reality at one point of time.

Ayemenem represents the pristine environment which is also true for India, but things changed with the coming of the colonials. The characters of the novel after sometime started losing their dreams. So did the Indians. Ayemenem did not act as a mute spectator; but it also started changing, not for the good of it but for the worse. The History House was a pristine countryside which never got a facelift and life also underwent a big change, but all this added to the misery of the people. Corruption became rampant in the society which was once free from this vice. People started to disbelieve each other and there was a breach of faith and man lost the sense of bonding, especially within the family.

Gradually, things changed to such a vastness that Ayemenem was no longer a countryside but a small township. Even though things around changed but still the people did not, their temperament did not and also the administration did not change. Things that changed were the surroundings – salt water barrage which regulated the flow of water from and to the sea. There was a time when the river was also able to change lives. But now it's all gone, the river has become just a green ribbon of slow-flowing stream that carried garbage and sewage to the sea. Upstream, the river had factory effluents which the author calls unadulterated. Ayemenem also had some five-star hotels but overall it had become a filthy paradise. So also was India, after the coming of the colonial forces the country lost all its past glory, grandeur and show. It became a place which had lost its past, lost its history and the pristine sense of beauty. Ayemenem has changed and so has India. The river has become polluted, so has the Indian society.

All the characters of the novel had a story to tell of its decadence. Ayemenem house or the History House had ruined itself. It saw the rise and fall of five contemporary generations, those who lived in it. The same thing is also true of India. It had also witnessed many upheavals. Ayemenem house and its occupants were known for their status that they maintained, but all was gone now. India in the olden days, before the arrival of the colonials, was a land that was quite known for its traditions and customs but it was all ruined in the postcolonial period. Along with the colonials came different ideas, which were completely foreign. Those ideas had completely changed the minds of the people of this vast country, which was governed by tradition and customs.

In this novel, which is a chronicle of lost dreams of each and every character, when we come across the oldest member of the Ayemenem house, we find suffering begins from Rev. E. John Ipe. In the initial chapter of the novel, Rev John is introduced. He was a priest of the Mar Thomas church. The process of suffering began with him when he got the greatest shock of his life, when his daughter Baby Kochamma defied his wishes and also declined to become a Roman Catholic. His sufferings continued unabated when he realised that his daughter cannot have a husband, as she had developed a reputation. He had sent her abroad and when she returned after two years, she was given the charge of the front garden. Rev. Ipe was a truly disappointed man only because of his daughter's fate. It was Baby Kochamma's mother who realised that Koh-i-Noor was none other than Baby Kochamma herself. For Baby Kochamma, life was 'a tale told by an idiot, full of sound and fury, signifying nothing'. Life was a total defeat for her; even she suffered in the hands of fate at the age of eighteen, when she fell in love with Father Mulligan, a young Irish monk. This monk was studying 'Hindu scripture in order to denounce them intelligently', which refers to the colonial feature of domination. This was one of the colonial attitudes as these forces used Christianity as a means to spread colonialism. It was yet another method of psychological domination of people's mind in the colonized territories. As the colonial theory goes, the Occidentals had come to India not only to rule over the Orientals, but also to teach the Indians as they were weak, feminine, and had no control over their emotions. In this novel, we find that Baby Kochamma in spite of knowing that monks are not allowed to make love or indulge in sexual acts, she could not resist her sexual emotions. Further, she made advances, clearly highlighting the lust and also had no control over emotions, which was one of the key factors of colonialism.

Finally, Baby Kochamma was withdrawn from the convent and sent abroad for studies. On her return after two years, she came along with new technology such as dish antennae, which brought into Ayemenem house wars, famine, football, sex, music, etc. The front garden under her charge wilted and had a natural death. Somehow she had developed a kind of mistrust in others, which happens to be another anti-colonial feature; this also made her keep the supplies under lock and key. Apart from other things, Baby Kochamma had also imbibed hypocrisy, which is revealed from her thought that 'her pursuance of herself regarding Mulligan was entirely due to her restraints and her determination to do the right thing'.

In the life of Baby Kochamma, there are ample examples of colonial attitudes. She as a child was also forced against her will to hold a red flag and wave it and say 'Inquilab Zindabad'. She had a typical stance regarding the downtrodden (The Paravan), the Untouchables – 'How could she stand the smell? Haven't you noticed? They have a particular smell, these Paravans' (p. 257). The same feeling and attitude was expressed by the colonizers for the colonized. In spite of all things said about Baby Kochamma, there are some lost moments in her life when she needs to be sympathized. She was seen gradually being reduced to an ordinary woman. It all happened after the death of Father Mulligan. She was a woman who lost her dreams at a very young age and that continued till she was eighty-three. In this novel, we have another dejected and defeated character. He happens to be a very minor and insignificant character, but still has an important role as far as personal suffering is concerned. He is Pappachi, the brother of Baby Kochamma. Pappachi suffers the greatest shock of his life when he realises that he has crossed the prime of life, whereas his wife is still young. This realisation almost breaks him. He was a retired government. official and considered making pickles below dignity. He expresses jealousy when his wife starts to be respected and honoured by others. That was one of the prime reasons for Pappachi to mercilessly beat Mammachi, but after Chacko his son came back from London, it stopped suddenly. He developed a psychological depression that Mammachi was neglecting him and thus his life had become miserable.

Pappachi was a man who dreamt of having something of his own, which he never wanted to share with anyone, not even with Mammachi or any member of his family. It was a sky blue Plymouth which he had brought from an Englishman. But this dream was also shattered with his death. The Plymouth passed on to Mammachi, Pappachi maintained a double personality. He donated money to orphanages and leprosy clinics, wanted people to look at him as a generous man with morality, but at home he was a real monster with his wife and children. Mammachi was yet another character in the novel who too had a shattered life. Although she too had dreamt of having a good and peaceful life, yet all went the other way round. Over and above, she was almost blind, which added to the misery of her life and almost uprooted her from the base. On familial and personal scale, she was a devastated lady who gradually developed a kind of harshness for life and all good things. Although Velutha, the Paravan, was able to provide the small pleasures of life to her daughter Ammu, Velutha created a kind of ripple in her mind. When she thought of him, she started to spit venom and bombarded her with all kinds of insults. The main reason for all this was a few of her unfulfilled dreams. Mammachi in a sense is just like the colonized who was destined to lead a lost life.

Mammachi's son Chacko was also one who suffered at the hands of his fate. He had been educated abroad, had a family and a nice daughter Sophie Mol, but for him life was a misery and a kind of dispensation. He always used to declare 'we are prisoners of war, our dreams have been doctored. We belong to nowhere, we sail unanchored on troubled seas, we may never be sad enough. Our joys never happy. Our dreams never big enough. Our lives never important enough. To matter' (53). This is what comes true of the colonized. They are a lot who are always looked down upon, and they are always trampled underfoot by the colonial's attitude. Chacko always had a colonial temperament in expressing things to be his, 'my factory, my pineapples, my pickles' (57). It is quite evident from the novel that Chacko had all the qualities of a dominant male and was truly a colonial by nature. Margaret Kochamma's father had a strong dislike for Indians and he believed Indians to be sly, dishonest people. Margaret Kochamma realized that she had married a wrong person and within a year she divorced Chacko and married Joe, her second husband, who had a sudden death. Her daughter Sophie Mol also had an unexpected death. Ammu is the most important character in the novel. She can be called the tragic heroine and she died at a very young age of thirty-one. Ammu started experiencing suffering at a very young age, when soon after her schooling she moved from Delhi to Ayemenem. She was denied an education by her father, which forced her to leave Ayemenem. After much reluctance, her father allowed her to go to Calcutta where she met her husband-to-be. Finally, she had a very elaborate marriage, but things changed rapidly as she found her husband to be a misfit, a liar and an alcoholic. Having no support from her husband, she found herself to be all alone. The manager of the tea plantation had an eye on her, and one day he suggested sending Ammu to the bungalow to be 'looked after'. Hence, she had to return, an unwelcomed entity into the Ayemenem house.

Velutha was the man who created a kind of sensation in her. He was the man who could give Ammu the small pleasures of life, something which Ayemenem house could not. There were certain things that happened near the house of Vellya Paapen, who, without realising the consequence, went to Ayemenem house to report. The end result: Ammu was locked inside a room. Meanwhile, Sophie Mol drowned. This gave way to further emotions and Ammu was driven out of the house. Ammu died in a dull, dark room in Alleppey. She died alone. In a way, Ammu was responsible for the next generation in the Ayemenem house, and all that happened there.

The twins Estha and Rahel had a totally wasted life. These twins projected their unity, and they always thought themselves as 'Me' and separately as 'We' or 'Us'. This is quite in contrast to the colonial theory of isolation, where they called themselves as 'Us' and the colonized as 'Other'. The greatest loss suffered by the twins was that they did not have a surname. It was again because of Ammu, who was thinking of reverting to her maiden name. The children almost had no scope of studies, while other children learnt what they had to learn, these twins were taught the basic traits of life and how history negotiates its terms and collects its dues from the breakers of law.

The children were taught lessons of mistrust, and even thoughts which are colonial. It was all because Ammu was afraid lest Estha should grow up like Chacko. Estha and Rahel were witness to the betrayal of a comrade by a fellow comrade, and also the brutal and merciless beating of Velutha which resulted in his death. Among the other members of the family, even Sophie Mol was not spared, and she had a life of tragedy. Sophie Mol is almost a dead character in the novel because she was introduced as 'dead' in the novel's first chapter. She was alive for a very short period of time.

The life of Sophie Mol was quite peculiar and she had two fathers, Chacko being the biological and Joe the unreal father. Chacko had to leave her early in life and Joe was killed in a car accident. Chacko could never create a place for himself in the mind of Sophie Mol. She was torn between these two fathers. It is also perceived that life seemed as a lost dream for many characters of the novel that were outside the arena of Ayemenem house. Apart from the members of the family, we also have some characters that are quite important and Velutha happens to be one such character. Velutha has been raised to the level of a tragic hero. He represented the 'Dalits' who are considered to be the most downtrodden class of the society. He was a serious Communist Party worker who had made many sacrifices, but when tragedy struck him, he did not get any help from his fellow partymen. He was badly beaten by the police and Estha and Rahel were mute witness to all that happened to him. His very name 'Velutha' was a contrast to his colour; Velutha means white in Malayalam, but Velutha was a dark-skinned man, a Paravan. Velutha, being a member of the Communist Party, thought himself to be a rebel and wanted to fight against the existing system to change it. Time played such a vital role that he was marked a real villain, humiliated in the hands of Mammachi, which was real torture and finally he was beaten to death by the police. Velutha is a well carved out character who lived only to see his dreams crash before being realized. It was Velutha's father Vellya Paapen who reported the acts of lust of his son, and that led to the whole tragedy.

Thus, *The God of Small Things* is a series of events in a society where there are different types of people, who have their own worries and problems. They have their failures of life within the family, lack of trust and self-respect. In the novel, we have a world of dreams that slowly grow up and also crash before being realized. There is a kind of relationship established among the various characters and Ayemenem house. Ayemenem house remains as a predominant motif for all the lost dreams of almost all the characters. Ayemenem was a place which had an oppressive atmosphere. This novel is a comprehensive protest novel, which highlights the atrocities against the powerless, the children, women and the Untouchables. Ammu is one such victim of the oppression just because she had her own way of leading life. This was the case with the 'other' class created by the 'us' class of people. Those who came here to this land of India came to rule upon and also to teach us the ways of life.

In Ayemenem, they danced to jettison their humiliation in the Heart of Darkness, their truncated swimming pool performances, their turning to tourism to stave off starvation. Ayemenem represents the History House whose history resembles that of India. The Indians danced to escape though for a brief period from the humiliation in the Dark Continent where darkness is a negative aspect of life. The Kathakali man is a typical character who can hide his inner feelings with a mask. He describes a story which he can very well handle – as he happens to be one of the characters and an indispensible part of the whole performance. This is somewhat similar to a colonial subject living in a postcolonial world.

The colonial subject was the one who had to suppress his emotions, feelings and ideologies because he is subject to oppression by the colonial forces. The story that the Kathakali man selects for his performance is that of the Mahabharata. Here, he has tried to enact the appearance of Karna and his stand in the great battle that was fought between the Kauravas and Pandavas. *The God of Small Things* is a story of shattered dreams from many points of view. We find almost all characters in a way exhibiting their helplessness about their loss. This is also true for the two main characters of the novel. Arundhati Roy has drawn a huge canvas and gradually the story unfolds one after another, five generations starting from Rev E. John Ipe to Sophie Mol. Although we have Rev John Ipe trying to have a good family, life was not smooth for Baby Kochamma. It was a kind of life in reverse gear for her. Pappachi and Mammachi were also not spared. They too had their versions of the tale of lost dreams. Chacko, the son of Pappachi and Mammachi, also had a tough time, struggling for a living and his sister Ammu was affected the most. Estha and Rahel, Ammu's twins, were kind of born to suffer. All the other characters, including Velutha, had some kind of suffering or the other. Thus, this sense of extreme loss makes the novel 'a saga of lost dreams'. The novel begins with a vivid description of the locale Ayemenem, to be precise the summer in Ayemenem. 'May in Ayemenem is a hot brooding month. The days are long and humid. The river shrinks and black crows gorge on bright mangoes in still, dustgreen trees. Red bananas ripen. Jackfruits burst. Dissolute blue bottles hum vacuously in the fruity air. Then they stun themselves against clear window panes and die, flatly baffled in the sun' (*The God of Small Things,* p. 1).

The novel proceeds to metaphorically symbolise the glory of India before the colonial period. It was Ayemenem which projects the image of India before the Raj. But gradually the characters of novel started to lose their dreams. The locale of Ayemenem was also subjected to change, just like its characters in the novel. Ayemenem was a typical countryside of Kerala, but gradually, the Gulf culture came in and it got urbanised. Lifestyle in the village changed. Small fish 'appear in the puddle that filled the PWD potholes on the highways' (*The God of Small Things,* p. 1) to add to the misery of the people who lived there! Now the banks of the river 'smelled of shit, and pesticides brought the World Bank loans' (*The God of Small Things,* p. 13). Around Ayemenem one could see the new, freshly-baked, iced, Gulf-money houses built by nurses, masons, wire-benders and bank clerks who worked hard and unhappily in far-off places. There was exploitation everywhere. The honest ration buyers were tempted by 'cheap soft-porn magazines about fictitious South Indian sex friends' with 'glimpses of ripe, naked woman lying in pools of fake blood' (*The God of Small Things,* p. 13).

It can be seen that the people had a different attitude towards life. They were ready to beat a bus driver to death; they can smash the windscreen of a car without any kind of hesitation and also venture out on the day of an opposition bandh. Police officers supposed to be the saviour of public life and property, had eyes which were 'shy' and 'greedy' and stared at the victim's breasts as they spoke and openly called a woman 'vashya', which meant 'prostitute'; this was not something peculiar to Ayemenem. In other words, there was a sea change in Ayemenem, the river which was once a life-giving source was polluted, the people had lost their innocence, concrete buildings had come up all round and it spelt the lost glory. Ayemenem could never think of going back to its old glory, similarly India had also changed a lot and lost its old glory. Ayemenem house or the History House also had a similar fate; it saw the rise and fall of the five generations who occupied it. The house was aloof-looking, 'it had little to do with people that lived in it' (165). The author has very skilfully used the image of an old man with rheumy eyes; 'like an old man with rheumy eyes watching children play, seeing only transience in their skill elation and their whole-hearted commitment to life' (*The God of Small Things,* p. 165). Further down the story, we find there are instances of downfall, downfall of people, material and the place as well.

In the novel, Roy talks of a Plymouth car, a symbol of a mythical takeover of the colonial power, because it was purchased from an Englishman by Pappachi. But it was an old car that simply stood as a silent witness to the fall of the History House that boasted of its pristine glory. All round Ayemenem and the Ayemenem house or the History House, we find signs of loss; 'Paradise Pickles and Preserves' that which was the pride of Ayemenem house was left with a signboard 'rotted and fell inwards like a collapsed crown' (*The God of Small Things,* p. 225). The so-called History House was empty, the doors, windows locked. 'Filth had laid siege to the Ayemenem house like a medieval army advancing on an enemy castle' (*The God of Small Things,* p. 88). Pappachi is another lost, dejected and defeated character of the novel. 'Paradise Pickles and Preserves' is where Rev. Ipe is introduced to the readers by the author. It was Rev. Ipe's daughter who gave him the first shock of life, when she defied his wishes to become a Roman Catholic. The first member of the third generation is Baby Kochamma, for whom life was just 'a tale told by an idiot, full of sound and fury, signifying nothing' (Shakespeare's *Macbeth,* 1969: 219).

Joseph Conrad in his book *The Nigger of Narcissism* (1965) writes, 'My task which I am trying to achieve is, by the power of the written word, to make you hear, to make you feel – it is, before all, to make you see' (5). In *The God of Small Things*, Arundhati Roy does the same thing, she makes us hear, feel and see for ourselves Baby Kochamma. Baby Kochamma was in love with Father Mulligan, a young Irish monk; at that time, he was in Madras. 'He was studying Hindu scriptures in order to be able to denounce them intelligently' (22). She tried her best to create interest in the mind of Father Mulligan for herself, but failed miserably.

Mammachi was a peculiar character; she was snobbish in many respects and also pretended that she had a great knowledge of literary works like *The Tempest*. She also enjoyed the way Ammu was punished because of her sins. But Mammachi was quite surprised by the development of the affair between Ammu and Velutha, the Untouchable. 'How could she stand the smell? Haven't you noticed? They have a peculiar smell, these Paravans' (*The God of Small Things,* p. 257). It is possible that the smell of an Irish monk was quite alright for her. But at the end, her endeavour was futile. Mammachi was a character who had suffered till the end and had some unfulfilled dreams.

Chacko, the son of Mammachi, is yet another character who could not live as he wanted to. According to him, life brought misery and desperation. 'We're prisoners of war, our dreams have been doctored. We belong nowhere. We sail unanchored on troubled seas. We may never be allowed ashore. Our sorrows will never be sad enough. Our joys never happy. Our dreams never big enough. Our lives never important enough. To matter' (*The God of Small Things,* p. 53). The sense of loss was so pervading that it also affected the children. It was quite evident from the fact that Estha and Rahel had no surname. It was all because of their mother Ammu considering a reversal to her maiden name. This created a kind of emotional crisis in the minds of the children. 'While children of their age learned other things, Estha and Rahel learned how history negotiates its terms and collects its dues from those who break the laws. They heard its sickening thud. They smelled its smell and never forgot it.

History's smell.
Like old roses on a breeze.

It would lurk forever in ordinary things. In coat-hangers. Tomatoes. In the tar on the roads. In certain colours. In the plates at a restaurant. In the absence of words. And the emptiness in eyes. That would grow up grappling with ways of living in terms of geological time it was an insignificant event. Just a blink of the Earth Woman's eye. That Worse Things had happened. That Worse Things kept happening. But they would find no comfort in the thought' (*The God of Small Things,* p. 55).

Last but not the least, Velutha was yet another character who is called *The God of Small Things* as well as the tragic hero of the novel. Characters who were outside the Ayemenem house or the History House had a different kind of life; for them, life was a lost dream. In this novel, the not so important character of the family develops into a tragic hero. He represents the Dalits who were the most underprivileged in the society. Velutha was a Communist Party card holder, but when tragedy struck, everything went upside down. He was mercilessly tortured to death. To conclude, we can say that the Ayemenem house or the History House symbolically represents the house of moral corruption and spiritual degeneration. The house was located in the middle of a rubber estate and belonged to Kari Saipu. 'A white man' is called Saipu in Malayalam, but in this novel Kari Saipu is 'The black Sahib'; he is 'Ayemenem's own Kurtz' (*The God of Small Things,* p. 52). Ayemenem has very willingly catered to all his dark passions, and the place was 'his private Heart of Darkness' (*The God of Small Things,* p. 52). This History House was witness to Kari Saipu's suicide, it also symbolized the horrors and discontents brought about by the advancing human civilization.

VI

According to some postcolonial theorists, postcolonial literature is the 'subversion' and resistance of the imperial 'centre'. For some theorists, it is an assertion of identity both in theme and language.

There is no doubt that postcolonial literature must be written in English, but it is no longer the Queen's English. Rather, it is the other English (or english) and it is this English which has given an identity to postcolonial literature. In the postcolonial era, postcolonial literatures are produced, which are written in varieties of 'englishes'. These may be regarded as the dialects of Queen's English, such as the African English, Caribbean English, Canadian English, Indian English, etc. Each variety of these 'englishes' has produced a substantial body of literature in the former British colonies.

In this sense, Arundhati Roy has successfully created a new Indian English idiom which distinguishes from the Queen's English and other 'englishes'. Ammu's love for Velutha is the central focus of the novel. The society was conservative and it laid down the rules as to who should love whom. The author argues that the right to love a man of her choice is a woman's birthright. It should not be vindicated in the name of religion, caste, colour and class. In this sense, this novel can be read as a feminist novel or a postcolonial novel, because the objective of feminism and postcolonialism is to break the old power structure. Arundhati Roy says 'it could be argued that it began long before Christianity arrived in a boat and seeped into Kerala like tea from a tea-bag. That it really began in the days when the love laws were made. The laws that lay down who should be loved, and how. And how much' (33). The 'love laws' is one of the most important themes of the novel *The God of Small Things*, and what the result is when they are broken. These 'love laws' are the set of principles and norms of society. These societal norms are so much ingrained in the people's psyche that they feel more like the laws of nature. Arundhati Roy has created a sense from children's affection for Velutha that they do not understand the notion of caste, which is deeply rooted in society and societal consciousness. By loving Velutha or by showing their affection for him in a way, they also broke the 'love laws'. Velutha's murder was again due to the breaking of these 'love laws' by their mother Ammu, who had an affair with an Untouchable.

Velutha's behaviour is unlike an Untouchable; this makes him conspicuous that he is too close to Estha and Rahel. Even his father thinks that he is crossing boundaries. Velutha was killed for breaking the 'love laws'; it was a conspiracy of sorts which led to his death. The children were also punished in the form of separation. Estha and Rahel after being separated for years are united during adulthood; they again break 'love laws'. Arundhati Roy reinforces this, that even though they were separated since ages but still they are 'two-egged' 'twins with Siamese souls'. The final word about the story is Ammu's 'Tomorrow', that which suddenly brings to one's mind the cliché that tomorrow never comes. Tragically, it does not for Ammu and Velutha.

Time and again Roy writes in the novel that 'things can change in a day'. The liberation from bondage and tradition can be possible not only by means of courage, but also by a new language. Therefore, the novel is experimental in terms of innovations of new coinages, new idioms and phrases like 'biological father', 'dieable age', 'sea secrets', 'rereturned', 'non-elect', 'death coiled like an angry spring', 'touchable', rice-Christians', 'clean children', 'like a packet of peppermints', 'as only as a wolf'. Moreover, the author combines the English and Malayalam language, showing us the hybrid nature that makes us think about the individual plight for identity. On page 196, the author suggests such types of hybridity in terms of language, 'thaiy, thaiy'.

In *The God of Small Things*, Arundhati Roy highlights how language becomes one of the key factors for domination for a nation as a whole or various social groups of a nation by any one dominant community. She also highlights the Indians' use of the language that was thrust upon them by the English; she further projects the idea with which the higher castes once under the English exercise their superiority over the lower castes to keep control. Homi Bhabha questions the idea of mimicry to be an act of paying homage to the colonizers. The word 'homage' indicates respect and a sense of admiration, but keeping in view the theories of language which clearly underline that perfection cannot be attained in the process of communication. Bhabha reveals how there is a kind of difference between what theory says and practical reality is. The outcome is that although it seems the adoption of the oppressors discourse is in reality a rejection of it:

> [T] he authority of that mode of colonial discourse that I have called mimicry is therefore stricken by an indeterminacy; mimicry emerges as the representation of a difference that is itself a process of disavowal. Mimicry is thus the sign of a double articulation; a complex strategy of reform, regulation and discipline, which 'appropriates' the Other as it visualises power. In the novel, we find a range of historical and literary allusions that either becomes a kind of ironical extension of the Colonizers or the Occidentals' negative perception of India. This allows comments on the narrowness of those who are subverted to take the opposite meaning in the novel. As regards the westernized returnees of their families, there is yet again an ironical use of almost all the historical or literary allusions quite similar to the use of western canonical texts hold in itself the appropriation of the Orient by the West. Roy, in her description, has widened her perspective beyond the Manichean opposition of interests and values. For example, the stone kangaroo that Rahel perceives to be real, living animal in reality presents a significant reading of the signposts. The sign that is swayed by the kangaroo symbol is that which indicates the taking over of the Indians with regard to their economy; in an all-out effort to their money. 'Kerala Development Corporation Welcomes You', and has a Kathakali dancer doing a Namaste (139). Further, Roy also highlights that Rahel notices two signboards at the airport, one of them was 'welcome to the Spice Coast of India' (39); this refers to the fact that Kerala was the first to have been colonized for trading purposes, and also that it is the coast through which Christianity and the Western world entered India. Rahel reads this backwards which also signifies the twins reading the police sign backwards when values are upturned and a man of innocence is killed in the name of maintaining 'morality'. This also indicates something more serious, Margaret Kochamma and her daughter Sophie Mol are not welcomed by Rahel and Estha. Both the twins have been forced by Chacko (their uncle) to speak in English, thereby making Sophie Mol's arrival associated with all sorts of

> unpleasant things and thoughts. There is a kind of hostile feeling in Rahel and she now gives a vent to all those by pinching Estha. 'Rahel, overcome by excitement and resentment, pinched Estha hard'. (*The God of Small Things,* p. 142)

All these events clearly indicate that Margaret Kochamma is going to enter a place which is no longer the spice coast which the English exploited, but which serves as a place for western tourists amid harmful smells of aids coming from the West.

As heredity would have it, profession passes on from generation to generation governed by the cast system. But the language features form a bridge between various castes. English language is the most powerful among all languages, it has a kind of dominant nature hence all the characters of the novel use it to assert their power over one another. This use of language helps the readers to read in a cheerful manner some of the events without giving scope to miss the humorous effects and also elevating the terrible nature, and the laughter evolved out of it, all the while having a distorted and hateful facial. The language used by the author also highlights the joyous moments of the children and their mother Ammu before experiencing the tragic events. According to Raja Rao, the 'Indians adopted the English language and adapted it to their local life, colouring it with their experience'. In *The God of Small Things*, Roy has tried to colour her language with the experience of the twins' perception and comprehension of the English rules. This projection of the children's experience by the author makes reading a pleasure, thereby allowing the reader to have an insight into the world of the twins. At one point of time through the narration, Rahel is scolded by Ammu, 'until Ammu shook her and told to stopit and she Stoppited'. Arundhati Roy has taken liberty with the language because of her love for the language and also her interest in making experiments for making amusing rhymes. 'Meeters from the Met, and Greeters from the Gret' (142).

Roy has purposefully used the device of flaunty spellings not only to project the Indian accent, but also to make a sarcastic remark on the attitude of some of the characters. For example, the speaking of the word 'divorce', 'Die-vorced', the word highlights the condemning attitude of a 'good' society for a divorced woman.

The word 'Die-vorced' projects something more than the usual. 'Die', according to Comrade Pillai, suggests a kind of barrenness because 'die' means having no issue from the first marriage. Further, Roy has made use of English in a peculiar manner; the English that Comrade Pillai speaks for instance is something quite absurd and hilarious, 'India-isms', this is to display a kind of mastery over the language used by the 'colonizers', 'My sister Sudha met with fracture sometime back' (*The God of Small Things,* p. 274).

Lenin had acquired a social position with a partial mastery of English. He boasted of his profession and also the material belonging; this is an accurate reflection of how far Indians can go in society through the evaluation of their English. The English that they spoke within the family was a means of projecting their authority since the use of this language gives one the impression of belonging to the colonizers clan. Baby Kochamma is a blind believer of western principles and made sure to point out to Margaret Kochamma that her family is a part of those people who partnered with the representatives of English colonialism. She also quoted William Shakespeare while narrating her family vanity. It is found very often in the novel that the twins are punished only because of their English. In a way, the use of the language is done as a means of exerting power, it is a symbol of power of the colonizers over the colonized. Baby Kochamma also imposed a fine on the twins, somewhat akin to the colonizers rewarding those who adopted the language, culture, the whole system with a livelihood.

The family that Arundhati Roy has projected in the novel is one of the respected families with a sound social and economic background. The family is quite conscious of the fact that it is behaviour and a certain pronunciation that makes it easy to trace the class and region to which one belongs. It can be evident from the way Ammu reproofs her children when they try and imitate their father's spit-bubbles. 'According to Ammu, only clerks behave like that, not aristocrats' (84). It is therefore clear that Ammu in spite of her association with a Dalit does classify people to some extent according to their behaviour. She has attributed 'vulgar' behaviour to 'lower classes'. For example, Inspector Matthews, whose language is a coarse version of Malayalam dialect; on the other hand, refined behaviour is always found with aristocrats.

The other members of the Ipe family take the mastery over English as a mark of status or a media to make people know that they are away from the masses. Ammu calls them Anglophile. They are also subservient to England, it serves as a criterion to classify themselves and people like Baby Kochamma and Chacko take recourse to quoting passages in English in his 'Reading Aloud voice' when he happens to be in his 'Oxford' 'Moods' (54). It is through the eyes of Chacko that we find England again trying to establish authority in the still colonized mind of his.

In one sense we can see the same weak ruler in Chacko who had allowed the country of India to come under the colonial rule, also providing ample scope to chain their own people. The story is narrated and projected in such a way that it symbolically represents India's surrender to the colonizers. All this is in the context of Chacko's modernization drive of the factory.

Baby Kochamma is known to have a superior feeling about herself over the other Indians only through her comparison of English with other beginners of English in the convent. She even at this age continues to compare herself with the British. It was on Margaret Kochamma's arrival in India that she could not control her emotions and excitement and started by saying that all the people waiting here at the airport are from the 'sweeper class'. The statement made by her puts her above the other Indians; further, this would also signify her class superiority just like the British (colonizers). Baby Kochamma although poses to be on top of the pyramid where the English stand, but her use of English is in a way ridiculed and also quite skilfully linked to the vacuum of her life. This emptiness is represented through echoes or repetitions that form the vital characteristic of the novel. In reality, in the attribution of the word 'pronunciation' to Baby Kochamma, the spelling is divided into syllables, 'Per Nun Sea ayshun' (154). This explains her condition as an ex-nun and is also a bitter comment on the futility of her sacrifice. The sacrifice of becoming a nun only to be closer to Father Mulligan, who had converted to Hinduism and also had become closer to other women, thus read 'a sea of nuns'.

To conclude, after reading the novel, one finds that to what extent the bourgeois assertion of claim of the two men was responsible for bringing down the hard work of the two women put in to earn a living for the family. It was both father and Chacko, the son, who dreamt of becoming the crème de Ayemenem. It was the father (Pappachi) who had quite symbolically bought an old car from an Englishman, as if to project the colonizing of the colonizers, an activity that would highlight his position to some authority. But, the car simply turns useless for want of activity and finally. It ends up stuck up in the ground. 'Like an angular, arthritic hen [...] with no intention of ever getting up' (295). Chacko also puts up a false vanity by putting up a signboard which has got nothing to do with him, as he does not participate in the actual work of pickling. The signboard faces the same fate as the car, it is now 'rotten and [fallen] inwards like a collapsed crown' (295). Therefore, the male chauvinistic symbol of superiority and caste, that which affected the family to a great extent, in a psychological collapse accompanied by economic failure. The novel also projects the re-writing of history officially. It is the narrator in the novel who uses a kind of inventive English language to defeat the right to a recognised space even for a hybrid or an 'outcast'. Salman Rushdie in his works, especially *Midnight's Children,* has made the world know the real use of Indian English. Arundhati Roy, on the other hand, makes use of the uniqueness of the language through the child's interpretation and understanding of the language. The children's use of the language and the adults' slow pace in front of the representatives of the white seems just a mockery of things. English is much more than a mere imitation or an appropriation of the colonizers' language. The language becomes a space within which meaning lives; the children feel and understand, still they are not moulded to any such shape by the environment they were in. It is therefore the 'children's' re-writing of their history and the history of their state Kerala takes on a new meaning as it rejects adult interpretations. This spreads throughout wasted ideas of liberty, honesty, jealousy, love and romanticism through the experience of the twins. The experience of life and nature, that which is narrated in a direct manner.

VII

Salman Rushdie has employed magic realist technique to redefine the novel *Midnight's Children* in a postcolonial context. He achieves this goal in terms of projecting the marginalized voices and histories of women and cultural minorities. Similarly, this trend can be noticed in Arundhati Roy's *The God of Small Things* in terms of the twins' subtle telepathy. Moreover, this is also noticed in Rahel's conviction that Sophie Mol is 'awake for funeral' in the first chapter. Besides these fantastic aspects of Arundhati Roy's writing, magic realism is employed by her as a stylistic device in terms of the heightened, imaginative perception of her child characters. One distinguishing feature of the postmodern and postcolonial literature is a combination of high and low cultural frame. For example, Arundhati Roy brings out the ironic interplay of the stories of the Mahabharata with more popular cultural references to cinema, television and advertising. This reminds us of American novels such as Don Delillo's *White Noise* (1985). Similarly, Arundhati Roy introduces the way in which the media such as television and film dislocate and marginalize the Ipe family. The concept of beauty and purity, which are inherent in Estha and Rahel's moral universe, are shaped and structured by their association with their lighter-skinned cousin Sophie Mol.

Arundhati Roy's experience of screen writing and film-making before writing *The God of Small Things* indicates that cinema is a great source of influence for her. This also happens in the case of

Salman Rushdie, whose reference to Bollywood cinema is found in his novel *Midnight's Children*. Similarly variety of cinema is referred in *The God of Small Things* and one is 'Chemmeen', a tragic South Indian musical romance. It is adopted by Ramu Kariat from the Malayalam novel by T.S. Pillai. The other is *The Sound of Music*, a Hollywood musical movie released in the same year (1985). It forms the basis of the Abhilash Talkies episode. Ammu listens to songs from 'Chemmeen' on her tangerine transistor radio. The blood of the film describes an unhappy married life of a fisherman and his wife and the failure of love between the fisherman's wife and her previous lover. This prefigures the affair between Ammu and Velutha. The local folk-myth in the figure of the 'seamother', whom the fisherman's community worships, prefigures Sophie Mol's death in the drowning of Palani. *The Sound of Music* reflects the childish aspirations and guilt which Rahel and Estha feel as a part of broken marriage. This is also perceived in case of Estha, who is the victim of sexual abuse. The film is a mixture of song, choreography and drama and its mountain scenery reflects the Indian elements. Similarly, 'Chemmeen' reflects the adult relationship in *The God of Small Things*. Arundhati Roy's adoption of a hybrid form of writing generates links with Rushdie's work. She is deeply rooted in the postcolonial tradition of Marquez and Rushdie. Like Rushdie, she makes use of such devices as extravagant capitalism, sentence fragments, paragraph breaks, and parenthesis, and metaphor transparency.

5 Constructing the Image of the Nation

Problems and Issues

The 1980s and 90s saw a renaissance of Indian Writing in English, with the emergence of authors like Salman Rushdie, Vikram Seth and Arundhati Roy. The renaissance was pioneered by Rushdie with his epochal and canonical novel *Midnight's Children* in 1981. Ever since his story of accomplishment, there has been a group of Indian authors making their significant contribution to Indian Writing in English. These contemporary authors are not only those people living in India, but like Rushdie, a large number of them are the part of the Indian diaspora. Earlier, writers like R.K. Narayan, Mulk Raj Anand and Raja Rao used English in its classical form. But Rushdie, with his innovative English, pioneered a new trend in writing and he voiced the multicultural concerns and issues. Next in the list is Vikram Seth, whose second book, *A Suitable Boy*, was based on post-Independent India. If Rushdie's work liberated Indian writing from the colonial straitjacket, Arundhati Roy's *The God of Small Things* radically changed the perceptions about Indian authors. Her book exemplifies postcolonial resistance by writing back in the language of the colonizer himself.

Rushdie's *Midnight's Children* intertwines the life of Saleem Sinai, the narrator of the text, with the socio-political development of

India as a nation after British rule. Saleem was born at the stroke of midnight as India gained independence. Saleem's destiny was tied up with that of India, and to a lesser extent, Pakistan and Bangladesh. Rushdie is a migrant author, whose diasporic consciousness has generated new ways of thinking about literature written by inhabitants of former colonies of the British Empire. *Midnight's Children* has generated critical response as to how we might think about literature that is written with cross-cultural dimensions. In the recent postcolonial study, there has been a thrust on certain fundamental issues as the loss of identity and imposition of new identities. Contemporary Indian diaspora writers deal with ethnic, cultural and political conflicts, which are giving new orientations to the already existing constructs of the West and the East. One fundamental characteristic of diaspora writing is the preoccupation with place, displacement and myths of identity. This trend has provided a unique status and identity to Indian diaspora literature of the contemporary age. The postcolonial studies have been concerned with several strands such as journey, migration, exile, return.

Salman Rushdie's *Midnight's Children* is hybridization between the resident and the diasporic consciousness. Rushdie is an expatriate Indian writer, who remarks in Imaginary Homelands:

> 'My novel *Midnight's Children*' was really born: when I realised how much I wanted to restore the past to myself … . What I was actually doing was a novel of memory about memory, so that my India was just that: 'My' India, a version and no more than one version of all the … possible versions I made my narrator, Saleem suspects his narration: his mistakes are the mistakes of fallible … and his vision is fragmentary. It maybe that when the Indian writer who writes from outside India tries to reflect that world, he is obliged to deal in broken mirrors, some of whose fragments have been irretrievably lost'. (*Imaginary Homelands*, pp. 10–11)

In *Midnight's Children,* Rushdie makes an attempt to review the history of his homeland, the community and family and depicts his diasporic consciousness. Even if he is an immigrant writer, he provides a comprehensive account of his homeland, as he has distanced himself by migrating to a foreign land. It is a comprehensive text that depicts Rushdie's nostalgic accounts of India's colonial and postcolonial history. The text is divided into three parts. Book I explores the incidents from 1915 onwards till Saleem is born at the stroke of midnight, 15 August 1947. Book II concentrates on his childhood and his role in Indo-Pak war in 1965. Book III deals with the Bangladesh war and the dark period of Emergency in India. Rushdie blends the national history with the domestic life of three generations of Sinai family, constantly moving to various parts of Indian Kashmir, Amritsar, Delhi, Agra, Bombay, and then to Karachi. This is how the novel connects the private life with the public life. In Rushdie's view, the lost identity can be recovered through memory. In *Imaginary Homelands*, Rushdie brings out the relation between an exile and his past. In his opinion, past is a foreign country from where we have all emigrated. So the only resort is to fictionalise memory. Literary creation is the only means to achieve it. In this sense, fiction is an alternative to official history which rejects the stories of the subalterns.

II

The comparison between Salman Rushdie's *Midnight's Children* and Vikram Seth's *A Suitable Boy* throws more light on their perception of the postcolonial reality in their texts. Just as Rushdie links the story of the Sinai family to the nation's story, Vikram Seth blends the story of Mrs Mehra's family with the history of post-Independent times of India as a nation. However, there is a perceptible difference in the approach to the political issues of the post-Independent period, which may be observed in their writings. For example, *Midnight's Children* celebrates the split of the polity, because it indicates the pluralism of democracy as opposed to the dictatorial discourse of Mrs Gandhi's regime. The culmination of this dictatorial discourse is manifested in Debakanta Baruah's slogan 'Indira is India and India is Indira'. On the other hand, the political scenario that Vikram Seth exemplifies is different from that of Emergency. *A Suitable Boy* provides the impression of a Nehruvian epic. He brings an account of Nehru's faith in secularism, which can suggest the only solution to the complex issues in the Indira scenario. Because the minorities like the Muslims and people of the lower caste were treated as the marginalised, being excluded from the traditional polity, the image of India that emerges in Seth's novel projects the history of post-Partition India and it concentrates on the profound concerns such as the inter-communal relations and the Zamindari system. Seth invents and constructs the image of India with its social history and its emphasis on postcolonial India. The subcontinent of this period is characterised by its different religions and languages, as it stands on the brink of its first general election. The novel has the epical dimension that touches upon the issue of Partition. More significantly, it deals with such issues that include national Indian politics in the period leading up to the election of 1952. Hindu-Muslim hostility, the status of the lower caste people, land reforms and the eclipse of the feudal princes and landlords, empowerment of Muslim women and academic affairs constitute the varied strands of the nation's image. The plot of the novel is set in the postcolonial India of the 1950s with its emphasis on the themes of inter-communal relations. In this sense, *A Suitable Boy* is a complex document of the postcolonial experience in its rejections of the Imperial British culture. The text deals with the problems of identity, such as the personal, religious and national, through a series of contrasts and contradictions. The whole gamut of the socio-cultural forces gives historical orientation to the lives of the characters. The sequence of episodes oscillates between individual attitude and cultural forces. Even individual lives are presented as the manifestation of the unconscious, operating as the symbolisation of the historical forces.

III

Like Rushdie and Seth, Arundhati Roy, in her novel *The God of Small Things,* blends the history of the Ipe family with the socio-political events of the state of Kerala, and implicitly with the contemporary history of the nation. Like many contemporary authors, Arundhati Roy draws on Indian mythic and narrative traditions. The influence of Rushdie's *Midnight's Children* on Arundhati

Roy is perceived in terms of the postmodern playfulness, the turn to history, a new exuberance to language, the reinvention of allegory and the reference to Bollywood. Besides Rushdie's work, the other source of influence for Arundhati Roy is the changes in India's political identity after Independence. Especially the threat to democratic freedoms during the Emergency of 1975–77, during which Mrs Indira Gandhi curbed the freedom of speech and jailed many of her political opponents. The other source of influence for her is maybe the growth of the dynamic and influential Indian 'diasporia' communities in the West. Arundhati Roy represents the diaspora as a state of the mind and it is not necessarily something to do with a political act of physical distancing from one's own country. In this sense, Arundhati Roy's *The God of Small Things* exemplifies a diasporization of fiction without any literal sense of diaspora. It refers to the desperation or separation of a group of people who belong to the same nation. This reflects the condition of alienation of the Anglo-Indians in India, which is represented by Sophie Mol in *The God of Small Things*.

Arundhati Roy has preferred to be influenced by Rushdie's pioneering role in establishing Indian English fiction as an international genre. *The God of Small Things* owes some of its formal and linguistic complexity to Rushdie's *Midnight's Children*. This is explicit when we encounter the child protagonists in both the texts. The plot of Rushdie's novel involves 1,001 children whose births coincide magically with the moment of India's independence at midnight on 15 August 1947. Rushdie's narrator Saleem 'tunes in' telepathically to the voices of the nation. He becomes the All India Radio for the other 'children of midnight'. Similarly, Arundhati Roy's twins, Rahel and Estha, share a more private psychic bond – a 'single Siamese soul' (p. 41). This kind of implicit unity allows Rahel to open the doors for her brother without hearing him knock and understand intuitively. Arundhati Roy acknowledges her debt to Rushdie in the pickle/chutney theme in *The God of Small Things*. This occurs when Mammachi writes to the manager of 'Padma Pickles' (a reference to a Bombay factory run by Rushdie's Saleem in *Midnight's Children* for advice on pickling techniques). In Rushdie's novel, pickles and preserves symbolise the fictional 'chutnification of history', which involves a highly political 'grand hope' of distilling the history of the Indian State. It also involves a migrant's desire to recapture the lost time and memories of home. Arundhati Roy's pickle theme plays on Rushdie's metaphorical association with history. This refers to the collapse of Mammachi's pickle business, which evokes the failure of the post-Independence generation to preserve the economic vision of a self-sufficient India. Of course, this vision was cherished by the leaders of the anti-colonial Indian nationalist movement, including Gandhi and Nehru.

Like Rushdie in *Midnight' Children*, Arundhati Roy is deeply interested in the relationship between personal lives and national events in the subcontinent. Her reference to 'Big God' of 'the vast, circling, driving, ridiculous, insane, unfeasible, public turmoil of a nation' recall the allegorical connections that 'handcuff' Rushdie's narrator Saleem to India's national history. For both the authors, these 'national allegories' are highly unstable and they are not presented as straightforward connections between the public story of the nation and the personal narrative. In Rushdie's *Midnight's Children*, Saleem, the everyman narrator, appears as a grotesque, cracked mirror of independent India. His story constantly struggles to accommodate itself to the story of the subcontinent, with its epic variety and dimension. On the other hand, Arundhati Roy restructures the epic mode to show a sense of integrity. This has been accomplished in terms of the expression of the personal despair of her protagonists. This personal despair is reverberated at different regional levels and national spheres.

The postcolonial texts like Rushdie's *Midnight's Children* and Arundhati Roy's *The God of Small Things* project such issues which are concerned with the struggle against imperialism. Moreover, such texts also involve the contradictions in the so-called independence nationalist movements. Arundhati Roy strongly attacks the post-Independence Indian government for its failure in fulfilling the needs of the common mass. Similarly, she undermines the national, caste and religious boundaries which still create wounds in the hearts of the people. At the same time, she provides some hope by suggesting that there must be more struggles for the cause of the marginalised sections of the Indian society. Arundhati Roy provides an elaborate picture of the environment of the castes and Syrian Christianity in postcolonial India. Her novel shows how globalisation is interconnected with the process of colonialism. She shows the impact of globalisation and colonialism on contemporary India. In her opinion, India as a nation has been shaped by globalisation and colonial policies.

IV

In *Midnight's Children*, Rushdie projects the image of India that exists at many levels. India may be understood as a dream, a collage of many colours, a blending of cultures, nationalities, and pluralistic society. He refers to the image of Lord Ganesh with a large nose and ears. This signifies the inherent urge for largeness, which is the typical Indian mindset. In this sense, Saleem Sinai represents the typical mindset, who constantly expresses his desire for the whole. India appears as a country of abundance, multiplicity, plurality, diverse customs and more. *Midnight's Children* is a postcolonial text that deals with ideas of nation and history. India as a nation is invented by the author and nation is defined as an 'imagined community'. Therefore, nation is fictionalised and narrated imaginatively in *Midnight's Children*. Rushdie dismantles the masters' house with the masters' own tools. Gone are the days when Bankim Chandra projected the image of the nation in his novel *Anandmath* in an idealistic and romantic way. On the other hand, contemporary authors like Salman Rushdie or Arundhati Roy or Vikram Seth have dealt with the idea of the nation in a more problematic way. Because various issues related to postcolonialism such as hybridity, hegemony, discourse and identity interplay with each other in constructing a complex image of the nation. The problematic areas are linked with Orientalism, Colonialism and Postcolonialism.

In order to achieve this goal, all these three authors are preoccupied with certain techniques, the evolving linguistic devices or the discourse. These novelists do not merely use English language as

English writers, but they transform the language and give it a distinct form or shape to suit their own purpose. In this context, the attempt undertaken by the novelists to experiment with the linguistic devices is a form of resistance to British colonialism. Arundhati Roy and Vikram Seth have made use of English language as one of the native languages. But actually, *Midnight's Children* is a path-breaking novel from this point of view, which has paved the way for the novelists of subsequent times. The use of English as a medium to narrate the nation implies a secularising discourse which helps these authors to construct and imagine the national community. It is a nation based on different religions, castes and languages. Salman Rushdie has made it clear that English should not be treated as something which is thrust upon by the colonial forces, but as something which is naturalised as any other Indian language. Arundhati Roy has gone far head in creating a new Indian English idiom that distinguishes it from the Queen's English and other 'englishes'. She insists that contemporary literature must liberate itself from the bondage and tradition by adopting a new language. Her experimental and innovative linguistic devices are manifested in the coinage of new idioms and phrases like 'biological father', 'die-able age', 'sea-secrets', 're-returned', 'non-elect', 'death coiled like an angry spring', 'touchables', 'Rice-Christians', 'cleanchildren', 'like a packet of peppermints', 'as only as a wolf'. Moreover, there has been a combination of English and Malayalam language, which shows the hybrid nature that throws light on the individual plight for identity. She shows the possibility that the complex form of hybridity can be presented in terms of a new-experimental language. Thus, it is quite inevitable that the postcolonial texts that deal with the construction of the image of the nation on the basis of hybridity and identity need to be written in an experimental language or discourse.

V

Besides the experimentation with the linguistic devices, Rushdie and Arundhati Roy have employed a magic-realist technique to redefine the nation in a postcolonial context. This brings a focus on the marginalised voices, histories of women and cultural minorities. According to Linda Hutcheon, the formal technique of magic realism, with its characteristic blending, has been used as a stylistic device by the postcolonial and postmodern writers. Rushdie's use of cinema in relation to India's culture is moulded by indigenous fiction and those of West. The events of the text also parallel the magical nature of the narrative, which is recounted in the *Arabian Nights*. In *Midnight's Children*, the narrative comprises and compresses Indian cultural history that includes the mythological narratives of Radha and Krishna, Rama and Sita, and they are coupled with the episodes of Romeo and Juliet. Similarly, this trend can be noticed in Arundhati Roy's novel in the twin's subtle telepathy. Rahel has the conviction that Sophie Mol is awake for funeral in the first chapter of the text. Besides most of the surreal or fantastic aspects, Roy's writing can be justified in terms of the highlighted imaginative perceptions of her child characters. The distinguishing feature of postcolonial and postmodern literature is a strange combination of the high and low cultural forms. For example, Arundhati Roy presents the ironic juxtaposition of stories of the *Mahabharata* with more popular cultural references to cinema, television and advertising. This reminds us of American novels such as Don Delillo's *White Noise*. This is the way in which the media such as television, films dislocate or marginalise the Ipe family. Roy's experience of screen writing and film-making before writing this novel has provided the necessary cue that cinema is a strong influence for her creative vivacity. Roy's adoption of a hybrid form of writing creates links with Rushdie's work. She is strongly rooted in the postcolonial tradition of Marquez and Rushdie. Unlike Rushdie and Arundhati Roy, Vikram Seth doesn't experiment with magic realism, but he makes use of classical realism, being influenced by Jane Austen, Tolstoy and George Eliot.

The experience of migration and diaspora has generated the recent trend of postcolonial literature. The literature produced by diaspora writers such as Amitav Ghosh, Bharati Mukherjee and Salman Rushdie signifies the exploration of the possibility of redefining the nation in their individual way. This has proved immensely popular in Western literary criticism and the critical theories established by Homi Bhabha, Avtar Brah, Rey Chow, Paul Gilroy and Stuart Hall. The novels written by Rushdie, Arundhati Roy and Vikram Seth explore the possibility of projecting the image of India in a more complex way, which is concerned with postcolonialism and postmodernism. In both cases, whether one is writing from outside the country or writing from within the country, he or she may reflect the diasporic consciousness, bring out a portrayal of the marginalised community and write the nation's history as an alternative to the official history that consists in recorded facts. These novels indicate that there cannot be one final version of history. History has many meanings and the meaning is determined by the present. In this sense, there shall be several versions of history as an ongoing process in keeping with the changing socio-economic political scenario, the heavy demands of novel writing as an evolving form, an experimental craft and the need for redefining and reinterpreting a nation's history.

Select Bibliography

Primary Sources

(A) Works by Salman Rushdie

This is a selective chronological list of works by Salman Rushdie.

Novels

Grimus. Great Britain: Gollancz, 1975.

Midnight's Children. Suffolk, UK: Picador, 1981.

Shame. United States of America: Alfred A. Knopf, 1983.

The Jaguar Smile: A Nicaraguan Journey. London: Viking Press/Penguin Books, 1987.

The Satanic Verses. London: Viking Press, 1988.

Haroun and the Sea of Stories. London: Viking Books, 1990.

The Moor's Last Sigh. London: Random House, 1995.

The Ground Beneath Her Feet. United States of America: Henry Holt & Company, 1999.

Fury. Great Britain: Jonathan Cape, 2001.

Shalimar the Clown. London: Jonathan Cape, 2005.

The Enchantress of Florence. London: Random House, 2008.

Luka and the Fire of Life. London: Jonathan Cape, 2010.

Essays and Interviews

Imaginary Homelands: Essays and Criticisms, 1981–1991. London: Granta in association with Penguin Books, 1992.

(B) Works by Vikram Seth

This is a selective chronological list of works by Vikram Seth.

Novels/Verse

Golden Gate. United States of America: Random House, 1986.
A Suitable Boy. New Delhi: Viking, 1993.
Equal Music. United Kingdom: Phoenix House, 1999.
Two Lives. India: Little Brown, 2008.

(C) Works by Arundhati Roy

This is a chronological list of works by Arundhati Roy.

Novel

The God of Small Things. New Delhi: India Ink, 1997.

Non-Fiction

The End of Imagination. Kottayam, India: DC Books, 1998.
The Cost of Living. New York: Flamingo, 1999. Contains the essays 'The Greater Common Good' and 'The End of Imagination'.
The Greater Common Good. Bombay: India Book Distributor, 1999.
The Algebra of Infinite Justice. New York: Flamingo, 2002. Collection of essays: 'The End of Imagination', 'The Greater Common Good', 'Power Politics', 'Ladies have Feelings, So ...', 'The Algebra of Infinite Justice', 'War is Peace', 'Democracy', 'War Talk' and 'Come September'.
Power Politics. Cambridge, London: South End Press, 2002.
War Talk. Cambridge, London: South End Press, 2003.
Ordinary Person's Guide to Empire. India: Penguin Books, 2004.

Secondary Sources

Ahmed, Aijaz. *In Theory: Classes, Nations, Literatures*. London: Verso, 1992.
Amin, Samir. *Neo-colonialism in West Africa*. Harmondsworth, UK: Penguin, 1993.
Ashcroft, Bill, Gareth Griffiths and Helen Tiffin. *The Empire Writes Back*. London: Routledge, 1989.
——. *The Post-colonial Studies Reader*. London: Routledge, 1999.
Armstrong, Nancy. *Desire and Domestic Fiction*. Oxford: Oxford University Press, 1987.

Atkins, Angela. *Vikram Seth's Suitable Boy: A Reader's Guide*. New York: The Continuum International Publication Group Inc, 2002.

Balakrishnan, Gopal (ed.). *Debating Empire*. New York: Verso, 2003.

Balvannandhan, Aida. *Arundhati Roy's The God of Small Things: A Study in Multiple Narratives*. New Delhi: Prestige Books, 2007.

Barry, Peter. *Beginning Theory: An Introduction to Literary and Cultural Theory*. New Delhi: Viva Books Private Limited, 2008.

Bassnett, Susan and Harish Trivedi. *Post-colonial Translation: Theory and Practice*. London: Routledge, 1999.

Bauman, Zygmunt. *Globalisation: The Human Consequences*. New York: Columbia University Press, 1998.

Bharat, Meenakshi. *Rushdie, the Novelist: From Grimus to the Enchantress of Florence*. New Delhi: Pencraft International, 2009.

Bharucha, Nilufer E. and Vilas Sarang. *Indian English Fiction 1980: As Assessment*. Delhi: B.R. Publication Corporation, 1994.

Bhabha, Homi K. *The Location of Culture*. London: Routledge, 1994.

——. 'Of Mimicry and Man: The Ambivalence of Colonial Discourse', in Frederick Cooper and Ann Laura Stoler (eds), *Tension of Empire: Colonial Cultures in Bourgeois World*, Berkeley: University of California Press, 1997, pp. 152–60.

Bhatnagar, Vinita Dhondiyal. *Reading in Indian English Literature: Nation, Culture and Identity*. New Delhi: Herman Publishing House, 2001.

Bose, Sujit. *Attitudes to Imperialism: Kipling, Forster and Paul Scott*. New Delhi: Amar Prakashan, 1990.

Bowers, Maggie Ann. *Magic(al) Realism*. New York: Routledge, 2007.

Brennan, Timothy. 'From Development to Globalisation: Postcolonialism and Cultural Studies', in Neil Lazarus (ed.), *The Cambridge Companion of Postcolonial Studies*, Cambridge: Cambridge University Press, 2003, pp. 120–38.

——. *Salman Rushdie and the Third World*. Basingstoke, UK: Macmillan, 1999.

Castle, Gregory (ed.). *Postcolonial Discourses: An Anthology*. Oxford: Blackwell, 2001.

Cesaire, Aime. *Discourse on Colonialism*. New York: Monthly Review Press, 1972.

Chatterjee, Partha. *Nationalist Thought and the Colonial World: A Derivative Discourse?*, London: Zed Books, 1996.

——. *The Nation and Its Fragments: Colonial and Postcolonial Histories*. Princeton, NJ: Princeton University Press, 1992.

Chrisman, Laura. 'Nationalism and Postcolonial Studies', in Neil Lazarus (ed.), *The Companion to Postcolonial Literary Studies*, Cambridge: Cambridge University Press, 2004, pp. 183–98.

——. *Postcolonial Contraventions: Cultural Readings of Race, Imperialism and Transnationalism.* Manchester: Manchester University Press, 2003.

Conrad, Joseph. *Heart of Darkness.* London: Blackwood's Magazine, 1902.

Cooppan, Vilashini. 'W(h)ither Post-colonial Studies: Towards the Transnational Study of Race and Nation', in Laura Chrisman and Benita Parry (eds), *Postcolonial Theory and Criticism,* Cambridge: D.S. Brewer, 2000, pp. 1–36.

Coronil, Fernando. 'Listening to the Subaltern: Postcolonial Studies and the Neo-colonial Poetics of Subaltern States', in Laura Chrisman and Benita Parry (eds), *Postcolonial Theory and Criticism,* Cambridge: D.S. Brewer, 2000, pp. 37–55.

Crane, Ralph J. *Inventing India: A History of India in English-Language Fiction.* London: Macmillan, 1992.

Davies, Tony and Nigel Wood. *A Passage to India.* New Delhi: Viva Books Private Limited, 2003.

Dey, Lal Behari. *Bengal Peasant Life.* Calcutta: Asia Publishing Society, 1874.

Dey, Pradip Kumar. *Salman Rushdie's Midnight's Children.* New Delhi: Atlantic Publishers & Distributors (P) Limited, 2008.

Dhar, T.N. 'History, Myth and the Postcolonial: The Indian Context', in Harish Trivedi and Meenakshi Mukherjee, *Interrogating Post-colonialism: Theory, Text and Context,* Shimla: Indian Institute of Advanced Study, Rashtrapati Nivas, 1996.

Dhawan, R.K. (ed.). *Postcolonial Discourse: A Study of Contemporary Literature.* New Delhi: Prestige Books, 1997.

——. *Arundhati Roy: The Novelist Extraordinary.* New Delhi: Prestige Books, 1999.

Dodhiya, Joydipsinh and Joya Chakrabarty (eds). *The Critical Studies of Arundhati Roy's The God of Small Things.* New Delhi: Atlantic Publishers & Distributors (P) Limited, 2001.

Dwivedi, A.N. and Amar Nath (eds). *Arundhati Roy's Fictional World of Collection of Critical Essays.* Delhi: B.R. Publishing Corporation, 2001.

Etherington, Norman. *Theories of Imperialism: War, Conquest and Capital.* New Jersey, USA: Barnes & Noble Books, 1984.

Fanon, Frantz. *Black Skin, White Masks.* Translated by Charles Lam Markmann (1952), New York: Grove Press, 1967.

——. *A Dying Colonialism.* Translated by Haakon Chevaliar, New York: Grove Press, 1965.

——. *The Wretched of the Earth.* 3rd edition, Translated by Constance Farrington, Harmondsworth: Penguin Books, 1990.

Fletcher, M.D. (ed.). *Reading Rushdie: Perspectives on the Fiction of Salman Rushdie*. Amsterdam: Rodpi, 1994.

Gandhi, Leela. *Postcolonial Theory: A Critical Introduction*. New Delhi: Oxford University Press, 2009.

Gillis, John (ed.). *Commemorations: The Politics of National Identity*. Princeton, NJ: Princeton University Press, 1990.

Gist, Noel P. and Anthony Gary Dworkin. *The Blending of Races: Marginality and Identity in World Perspectives*. USA: John Wiley & Sons Inc, 1972.

Hall, Stuart. 'Race, Articulation, and Societies Structured in Dominance', in *Sociological Theories, Race and Colonialism*, Paris: UNESCO, 1980, pp. 305–45.

——. 'When was the 'Postcolonial'? Thinking at the Limit', in Iain Chambers and Lidia Curti (eds), *Post-colonial Question: Common Skies, Divided Horizons*, New York: Routledge, 1996, pp. 242–60.

Harrison, James. *Salman Rushdie*. New York: Twayne Publishers, 1992.

Harrison, Nicholas. *Postcolonial Criticism: History, Theory and the Work of Fiction*. Cambridge: Blackwell, 1989.

Harvey, David. *The New Imperialism*. Oxford: Oxford University Press, 2003.

Herwitz, Daniel and Ashutosh Varshney, *Midnight's Diaspora Encounters with Salman Rushdie*. New Delhi: Penguin Group, 2009.

Hobsbawin, E.J. *The Age of Imperialism*. London: Weidenfeld & Nicolson, 1987.

Hogan, Patrick Colm. *Colonialism and Cultural Identity: Crisis of Tradition in the Anglophone Literatures of India, Africa and the Caribbean*. Albany: States University of New York Press, 2000.

Huggan, Graham. *The Post-colonial Exotic: Marketing the Margins*. London: Routledge, 2001.

Hutcheon, Linda. *A Poetics of Postmodernism: History, Theory, Fiction*. London and New York: Routledge, 1988.

——. *The Politics of Postmodernism*. London and New York: Routledge, 1989.

——. *Rethinking Literary History: A Forum on Theory*. New York: Oxford University Press, 2002 (with Mario J. Valdes).

——. *A Theory of Adaptation*. New York and London: Routledge, 2006.

Jain, Jasbir and Veena Singh (eds). *Contesting Postcolonialism*. New Delhi: Rawat Publications, 2000.

Jain, Jasbir. *Beyond Postcolonialism: Dreams and Realities of a Nation*. New Delhi: Rawat Publications, 2006.

Jameson, Frederic and Masao Miyoshi (eds). *The Cultures of Globalisation*. Durham, NC· Duke University Press, 1998.

Kaplan, Caren. *Questions of Travels: Postmodern Discourses of Displacement*. Durham, NC: Duke University Press, 1996.

King, Richard. *Orientalism and Religion: Postcolonial Theory, India and the Mystic East*. London: Routledge, 1999.

Kipling, Rudyard. *Kim*. New Delhi: Indialog Publications Private Limited, 2003.

Kortennar, Neil Ten. 'Midnight's Children and the Allegory of History', *Ariel*, 26 (1995).

Kumar, T. Vijaya, Meenakshi Mukherjee, Harish Trivedi and C. Vijayasree. *Focus India: Postcolonial Narratives of the Nation*. New Delhi: Pencraft International, 2007.

Lazarus, Neil. *Nationalism and Cultural Practices of the Postcolonial World*. Cambridge: Cambridge University Press, 1999.

Lewis, Reina and Sara Mills (eds). *Feminist Postcolonial Theory: A Reader*. Edinburgh: Edinburgh University Press, 2003.

Lodge, David. *The Art of Fiction*. London: Penguin Books, 1992.

Loomba, Ania. *Colonialism/Postcolonialism*. London: Routledge, 1998.

Loomba, Ania, Suvir Kaul, Matti Bunzl, Antoinette Burton and Jed Esty (eds). *Postcolonial Studies and Beyond*. New Delhi: Permanent Black, 2008.

Lye, John. 'Some Issues in Postcolonial Theory', in *Contemporary Literary Theory*, Ontario: Brock University, 1997.

Marquez, Gabriel Garcia. *One Hundred Years of Solitude*. New Delhi: Penguin, 1996.

McLeod, John. *Beginning Postcolonialism*. New Delhi: Viva Books, 2010.

Meyers, Birgit and Peter Geschiene (eds). *Globalisation and Identity: Dialectics of Flow and Closure*. Oxford: Blackwell, 1999.

Michael, Edwardes. *British India 1772–1947: A Survey of Nature and Effects of Alien Rule*. London: Sidgwick and Jackson, 1967.

Mignolo, Walters. *Local Histories/Global Designs: Coloniality, Subaltern Knowledge, and Border Thinking*. Princeton, NJ: Princeton University Press, 2000.

Mohapatra, H.S. and J.K. Nayak. 'Farewell to Jane Austen: Uses of Realism in Vikram Seth's A Suitable Boy', in Y. Park and R. Sunder Rajan (eds), *The Postcolonial Jane Austen*, London: Routledge, 2005.

Mohapatra, H.S. 'Riches of India: Reading Vikram Seth's A Suitable Boy', in Viney Kirpal (ed.), *The Postmodern Indian English Novel: Interrogating the 1980s and 1990s*, Bombay: Allied Publishers, 1996, pp. 41–48.

Mongia, Padmini (ed.). *Contemporary Postcolonial Theory: A Reader*. New Delhi: Oxford University Press, 1997.

Mukherjee, Meenakshi (ed.). *Rushdie's Midnight's Children: A Book of Readings*. New Delhi: Pencraft International, 1999.

Mukherjee, Meenakshi. *The Twice Born Fiction: Themes and Techniques of the Indian Novel in English*. London: Heinemann, 1971.

——. *The Perishable Empire*. New Delhi: Oxford University Press, 2000.

Naik, M.K. and Shyamala Narayan. *Indian English Literature 1980–2000: A Critical Survey*. New Delhi: Pencraft International, 2001.

Naipaul, V.S. *An Area of Darkness*. London: Picador, 1995.

Narasimhaiah, C.D. *Essays in Commonwealth Literature: Heirloom of Multiple Heritage*. New Delhi: Pencraft International, 1995.

Navarro-Tejaro, Antonia. *Gender and Caste in the Anglophone-Indian Novels of Arundhati Roy and Githa Hariharan: Feminist Issues in Cross-Cultural Perspectives*. USA: Edwin Mellen Press, 2005.

Nicholas, Kai. *A Perspective of Social Problems: Indo-Anglian and Anglo-Indian Novels*. Bombay: Jaico Publishing House, 1972.

Pandey, K.M. 'The Small God Made Big: Arundhati Roy's The God of Small Things', in R.K. Dhawan (ed.), *Indian Women Writers*, New Delhi: Prestige, 2001, pp. 172–79.

Pathak, R.S. (ed.). *The Fictional World of Arundhati Roy*. New Delhi: Creative, 2001.

Panwar, Purabi. 'Kipling's Fictional India: The Traveller and His Plain Tales', in *India in the Works of Kipling, Forster and Naipaul: Postcolonial Revaluations*, New Delhi: Pencraft International, 2000.

Parameshwaran, Uma. 'Handcuffed to History, Salman Rushdie's Art', *Ariel*, 14 (1983): 34–35.

——. *The Perforated Sheet: Essays on Salman Rushdie's Art*. New Delhi: Affiliated East-West Press, 1988.

Prakash, Gyan (ed.). *After Colonialism: Imperialism Histories and Postcolonial Displacements*. Princeton, NJ: Princeton University Press, 1995.

Prasad, Murari (ed.). *Vikram Seth's A Suitable Boy: An Anthology of Recent Criticism*. New Delhi: Pencraft International, 2005.

Prasad, Murari. *Articulating the Marginal: Arundhati Roy's Writings*. New Delhi: Pencraft International, 2006.

——. 'Understanding Seth', a review of *Vikram Seth: An Anthology of Recent Criticism*, G.J.V. Prasad (ed.), New Delhi: Pencraft International, 2005.

——. *Arundhati Roy: Critical Perspectives*. New Delhi: Pencraft International, 2006.

Rajagopalachary, M. and B. Krishna Keerthi. 'Social Realism in Vikram Seth's A Suitable Boy', *Kakatiya Journal of English Studies (Warangal India)*, 20 (2000): 101–10.

Rao, Raja. *Kanthapura*. Delhi: Oxford University Press, 1998.

Said, Edward W. *Culture and Imperialism*. Great Britain: Vantage, 1993.

——. *Orientalism: Western Conceptions of the Orient*. New Delhi: Penguin, 2001.

Sanga, Jaina C. *Salman Rushdie's Postcolonial Metaphors*. Westport, CT: Greenwood, 2001.

Singh, A.K. 'Vikram Seth's A Suitable Boy: A Critique', in R.S. Pathak (ed.), *Indian Fiction of the Nineties*, New Delhi: Creative Books, 1937.

Singh, Kushwant. *Train to Pakistan*. New Delhi: Time Books International, 1989.

Sharma, R.S. and Shashi Bala Talwar. *Arundhati Roy's The God of Small Things: Critique and Commentary*. New Delhi: Creative Books, 1998.

Selmon, Stephen. 'Magic Realism as Post-colonial Discourse', *Canadian Literature*, 116 (1988): 9–24.

Srivastava, Neelam. 'Midnight's Children and A Suitable Boy: Challenges of Rendering Indian Experiences into English', in Murari Prasad (ed.), *Vikram Seth's A Suitable Boy: An Anthology of Recent Criticism*, New Delhi: Pencraft International, 2005.

Stiglitz, Joseph. *Globalisation and Its Discontents*. New York: Norton, 2002.

Surendran, K.V. *The God of Small Things: A Saga of Lost Dreams*. New Delhi: Atlantic Publishers & Distributors (P) Limited, 2007.

Thieme, John. *The Arnold Anthology of Post-colonial Literatures in English*. London: Arnold, 1996.

Trivedi, Harish and Meenakshi Mukherjee (eds). *Interrogating Post-colonialism: Theory, Text and Context*. Shimla: Indian Institute of Advanced Study, Rashtrapati Nivas, 1996.

Vishwanathan, Gauri. *Masks of Conquest: Literary Study and British Rule in India*. London: Faber, 1990.

Walsh, William. *Indian Literature in English*. England: Longman, 1990.

Willam, Patrick and Laura Chrisman (eds). *Colonial Discourse and Post-colonial Theory: A Reader*. New York: Columbia University Press, 1994.

Index